# Memories

# Memories

Satsvarūpa dāsa Goswami

GN Press, Inc.

Persons interested in the subject matter of this book are invited to correspond with our secretary:

GN Press, Inc.
R.D. 1, Box 832
Port Royal, PA 17082


Printed in the United States of America
ISBN 0-911233-69-5

GN Press gratefully acknowledges the BBT for the use of verses and purports from Śrīla Prabhupāda's books. 

# Contents


| | |
|---|---|
| Author's Note | 1 |
| Introduction | 3 |
| A Chronological Sketch | 6 |
| Saint Or Sinner? | 11 |
| Bay Terrace | 13 |
| Nail-biter | 16 |
| Father | 19 |
| Our Memories, Our Truths | 22 |
| Emotion Evoked by Jazz . . . | 24 |
| When To Fight | 25 |
| The Past Leaks Into The Present | 29 |
| Epiphanies | 32 |
| Blackberry Picking | 34 |
| Spring Potpourri | 36 |
| Spiritual Aspirations | 38 |
| An Act Of Faith | 41 |
| Competition Among Godbrothers | 43 |
| Memory As Political | 45 |
| Garden Seat | 49 |
| Pain | 51 |
| Remembering The Divine Spark . . . | 54 |
| Father And Prabhupāda | 56 |
| We Have Changed For The Better | 58 |
| Joie De Vivre | 61 |
| "But Trailing Clouds Of Glory . . . " | 63 |

Places 65
Perpetual Motion 68
Who Cooked For Kṛṣṇa . . . 71
At The Time Of Death . . . 74
Re-reading The Early Chapters . . . 76
Valuing Memories . . . 80
"My Trade And My Art . . . " 82
I Was Drowning 86
He Is God For Me 88
Memories Of Death 89
The Strand Theater . . . 93
O Daughters, O Sons 96
Calamities 98
My First Visit To 26 Second Avenue 100
Mentors 104
Looking Into The Dark 106
Remembering The Teachings . . . 109
The End 111
My Intention To Remember 121
Irish Devotees 124
We Are Family 126
Don't Be Ashamed Of Love 128
Do You Remember In Ireland When—? 130
A Defense Of Memories 132
Madeline 137
Free-write Memory 142
Mom, You're An Ace 148
Perspectives Of Memory 150
Mādhava dāsa's Memories 153
Past, Present, And Future 156
Diving Out The Window 158

This Self In This Body . . . 161
Overcoming Regrets . . . 163
Why I Don't Dwell . . . 167
Tuscarora Creek 170
Vocation As A Writer 172
Why I Didn't Become A Father 178
Proud Of Prabhupāda 181
Spiritual Fantasies . . . 182
He Needs Fighters 184
God Remembers 186
Preserving The Record 189
First Impressions Of Prabhupāda 194
Young Friends 197
I Shouldn't Be Here 198
Free Spirit 200
A Lesson 202
Those Days And These 204
Blurred Neons 206
Not Better Nor Worse 209
How I Wish To Be Remembered 211
A Last Recognition 213
Little Life 214

Glossary 217
Acknowledgments 227

# Author's Note

The inspiration for *Memories* and the freedom to write it was given to me by Lord Kṛṣṇa and Śrīla Prabhupāda while residing in the ISKCON community in Wicklow, Ireland. This book is not an autobiography but a compilation of independent pieces or vignettes, each with its own title. While both the pre-Kṛṣṇa conscious memories and memories since 1966 flowed, I encountered the usual obstacles. I overcame these obstacles by discussing in separate pieces the nature of memory and a defense of reminiscence in the life of a practicing devotee.

I deliberately avoided ordering the memories chronologically. Some of the memories repeat and recur, such as two similar memories in this book where I tell about my mother and her rejection of me. The possibility of separate and recurring memories from a lifetime separated into pre-Kṛṣṇa conscious and ISKCON memories has, I think, the potential to be developed in future volumes. There's no harm in remembering the same events and then looking at them from different points of view as we grow older and gain new insights.

After working alone at *Memories* for a week, I turned to the approximately twenty devotees in Wicklow and asked them to help me. At first, I asked them to write me notes requesting memories from my life in which they were interested. The devotees responded enthusiastically and some of their requests are included here. A few days later, I then made another request: I asked them to relate one of their own memories, but one in which I was present. I then used these reminiscences to springboard into my own remembrance of the same event.

As I completed *Memories* and was about to leave Wicklow, the devotees presented me with a Sheaffer pen on which was inscribed, "*Memories*, S.D.G., Wicklow, 1996."

I asked my editor to retain the names of both the devotees I remembered and of those who submitted their memories, so don't be surprised if you see familiar names. My editor boiled down the manuscript so that fifty percent of what I wrote is presented here for your reading, focused on the process of memory and what it means.

I now invite you to read this book and I hope that you will agree with my concluding lines, "We are fortunate to be in this river of important considerations called the Kṛṣṇa consciousness movement. Anywhere we dip in, we come up with a handful of Ganges water. Don't sell it short."

# Introduction

Some people are strong advocates of memory as a spiritual tool. When Marcel Proust dipped his cake into his tea, a flood of memories washed over him, associations from his past. Similarly, when a devotee is Kṛṣṇa conscious, the sight of a peacock fan can throw him into a whole remembrance of Kṛṣṇa.

Well, that doesn't happen to me so much. Is all we have, then, a laughable life? I want to assert that our lives and memories are valuable because they lead to Kṛṣṇa consciousness, just as when we follow the course of the Gaṅgā, we eventually flow into the Yamunā and arrive in Vṛndāvana. We have memories of guru and memories of our attempts to approach Kṛṣṇa, although we often fell short. We might think of approaching the Deities, and we suddenly remember that these Deities are the most beautiful forms of Kṛṣṇa in the world. We feel excited to see Them. Then when we do see Them, we come face-to-face with our lack of devotion; we don't feel as much as we would like to. Those are the inevitable limits of our inevitably real lives. We plan something, and inevitably it is curtailed by our own inability or by the forces of nature. What is the use of remembering all those incidents? Are such memories part of reality or illusion? If we omit all those factors that stopped us from expressing love or service and remember only the apparently positive aspects of our lives, does that make our lives more real? I don't think so.

Memory should be relentless and accurate. It is important to remember our actual feelings. If we felt emptiness instead of *bhāva* as we stood in front of the Deities, or felt relief and a resurgence of faith, why not claim that as genuine to our experience? I remember bowing down once at New Māyāpur. I first approached Gaura-Nitāi, then Rādhā-Govinda-Mādhava, then Kṛṣṇa-Balarāma. Although I saw Govinda-Mādhava's beautifully accentuated *tribaṅga* pose, I felt particularly moved by the look in Kṛṣṇa-Balarāma's eyes as They glanced straight in front of Them, maybe seeing the demons coming on the horizon. I prayed to Them at that time to chasten me and protect me. This actually happened to me.

Admittedly, memories even of our Kṛṣṇa conscious life are of temporary situations. Again a memory from New Māyāpur: I went there several times in autumn, the season when the chestnuts break out of their shells and lay on the ground like drops of beautifully varnished mahogany. You're just drawn to pick them up and hold them for a few minutes, they're so beautiful. As I walked in the woods there with the leaves falling from the trees around me, I planned what I would do with the rest of my year and what books I would write and publish in service to Prabhupāda.

It's a memory, but it's of temporary life spent in Kṛṣṇa consciousness in a world that will also pass away. Despite its fleeting nature, however, Kṛṣṇa assures us that whatever devotional service we perform is never lost. It is to our eternal credit, and it accumulates life after life until we are so full of devotion we go back to Godhead. In that sense, these memories are not just remembrances to please the false ego, but hope for our future as devotees. They are proof that our credits are being counted. Anyone can read them and feel safe in their own devotional practices. In fact, even hearing of another devotee's devotion, no matter how small, creates more credit for ourselves. Therefore, to hear about Kṛṣṇa and Kṛṣṇa's devotees makes us happy.

We all feel the urge within ourselves to acknowledge our own existence and even to celebrate it in relation to Kṛṣṇa. I think we can feel confident that Kṛṣṇa is behind everything, and that if we try to see Him there—in the world and in ourselves, in our memories—we will be successful.

# A Chronological Sketch

They say we are what we were. I can't claim to be plumbing the depths of my life enough to tell you who I was or how I lived, but there is an obvious timeline in my life that I would like to sketch while it's on my mind.

The first division goes from birth to the age of twenty-six. This is my life before I met Prabhupāda. Within those twenty-six years, there are subdivisions, such as being my parents' child, then gradually rebelling and developing my own life through college, friends, and hip culture, then the Navy, and finally the Lower East Side.

After 1966, everything changed. Before 1966 I was alienated—because of the type of person I was—from mainstream American culture. I identified more with the growing minority of sensitive writers, artists, musicians, and marijuana-smokers. After I met Prabhupāda, my alienation became more widespread: I became set apart from everyone who was not a devotee of Kṛṣṇa. I now lived in the ISKCON world, which although insular, was not completely isolated from the people to whom we preached.

That second segment of my life runs from 1966–1977 and it is the time when I was entirely absorbed by ISKCON's mission. Although I was married for a few years, then took *sannyāsa*, I lived that whole period focused on living the Absolute Truth according to ISKCON's definition of it and trying to give the world all or at least some of my understanding of what that meant.

After Śrīla Prabhupāda's disappearance, everything changed again not only for me but for all ISKCON devotees. For the sake of this timeline, however, I would call the next nine years the zonal *ācārya* years. During those years, I lived in the special consciousness that I was one of the exclusive eleven gurus chosen to lead the society. For better or worse, ISKCON—and I—continued on with the same premises: that is, that we had the Absolute Truth and that we had nothing more important to do than to share it with those who did not have the Absolute Truth. During this period, I continued as a member of the GBC, a position that gave me both special burdens and special privileges.

The next segment began in 1986 when I decided to resign from the GBC. This is also around the time when I accepted that my headaches were chronic and that I would have to adjust my life to accommodate them. I'm still in this period. This is the time when I am trying to discover who I am. The major change is that although I am certainly still within ISKCON, I am no longer on the front lines as I used to be. ISKCON has changed and I'm sure the nature of the GBC has changed with it, but I am now a private citizen in ISKCON, and I seek to make my own path, especially as a writer and an artist in Kṛṣṇa consciousness.

I was just leafing through Virginia Woolf's memoir, *A Sketch of the Past*, in which she captures her earliest memories and then analyzes her relationship with her mother. I was amazed at how she can be so conversant and expressive about her life. It occurred to me that our lives as devotees are harder to define. My timeline shows that my life is divided into two main parts, two separate selves: pre-Kṛṣṇa consciousness and life after I joined ISKCON. Those divisions tend to be rather absolute; they are our B.C. and A.D., our "second birth." The past is a "past life." Sometimes people ask me where I was born. Instead of saying I was born on December 6, 1939 in New York City, I tell them I was born in the summer of 1966 at 26 Second Avenue. Everything that came after that birth has been radically different from my life before that date. What makes it difficult, however, is that the jump from 1965 to 1966 is so drastic that it has become a kind of barrier. Am I what I was, or something different? Was that "past life" me, or someone different? The memories of those pre-Kṛṣṇa conscious days seem to be mine, and they continue to spill into my life in the present.

Virginia Woolf makes an almost similar point when she describes how her mother died when she was thirteen. She says that her mother's death changed her life so completely that it wasn't until she was in her forties that she was able to finally let her mother go. I say "almost similar" because the change that takes place in the life of a devotee does not have to be exorcised. It is the beginning of our real lives.

At the same time, our lives after we joined the movement bear examining. Those first eleven years after I met Prabhupāda were intense because Prabhupāda was present and our ISKCON family was growing. After 1977, my life continued in a somewhat lost and chaotic way, although it was still dedicated to Prabhupāda in separation.

There is also another factor by which we can examine our experiences. That is, as Virginia Woolf points out, by the influence others have over our lives even when they are absent. She's not talking so much of people with whom we work, but those with whom we become obsessed.

> This influence, by which I mean the consciousness of other groups impinging upon ourselves; public opinion; what other people say and think; all those magnets which attract us this way to be like that, or repel us the other and make us different from that; has never been analysed in any of those Lives which I so much enjoy reading, or very superficially.
>
> Yet it is by such invisible presences that the "subject of this memoir" is tugged this way and that every day of his life; it is they that keep him in position. Consider what immense forces society brings to play upon each of us, how that society changes from decade to decade; and also from class to class; well, if we cannot analyse these invisible presences, we know very little of the subject of the memoir; and again how futile life-writing becomes. I see myself as a fish in a stream; deflected; held in place; but cannot describe the stream.

When I think of "social" pressure, I think of how the GBC members and other prominent ISKCON leaders have affected me even though I wasn't working closely with them. If I didn't know their opinions, I would create them, imagine them, and carry them with me. These "presences" became real in just the way Woolf describes. Therefore, I can't claim to know myself unless I understand how these different forces work on me. That includes the world of nondevotees.

I prefer to think that my life has been shaped completely by my spiritual master, but is that true? It would really depend on to what degree my love for him is genuine. How can I know, minute to minute, whether or not he is pleased with me? All I can do—all I *do* do—is maintain an abiding faith that he is my ever well-wisher. Does he know the depths of my nature? I don't always know. Perhaps it doesn't matter. He knew me well enough to pull me free.

Looking back, Virginia Woolf realizes that because her mother had seven or eight children and many other duties, she couldn't possibly have spared attention for one child. Woolf says that she hardly remembers ever having her mother's exclusive attention; someone was always interrupting. Her mother was the center of their lives, but in a general way. " . . . I see now that a woman who had to keep all this in being and under control must have been a general presence rather than a particular person to a child of seven or eight." I sometimes felt like this in my relationship with Prabhupāda when his seven or a dozen children became four thousand.

There's a nice moment in Woolf's memoir when she tells us the last words her mother spoke to her: "And there is my last sight of her; she was dying; I came to kiss her and as I crept out of the room she said: 'Hold yourself straight, my little Goat.'"

Such a personal touch at the end. I hope Prabhupāda remembers me as his small servant and that I will rejoin him when I leave this world. That would be the fitting end to my timeline and it is the one hope I hold dear in telling my memories. A devotee's memoir is not a description of his mortality, but of his immortality in the making.

# Saint Or Sinner?

We pare from our lives anything that is not Kṛṣṇa conscious. Therefore, it is natural to remember those things that we did during our Kṛṣṇa conscious practices and to forget the rest. Yet some of those other memories must remain because we want to make a truthful testament. We don't want to be guilty of self-hagiography, or turning ourselves into ideal saints. We have seen a few such treatments written by Śrīla Prabhupāda's grand-disciples about their initiating gurus. Although it is true that Prabhupāda's disciples were all fortunate objects of his mercy, it is also true that most of them underwent conversion between the ages of sixteen and thirty. When we read that their guru showed spiritual tendencies since childhood and that his childhood was like no other childhood, we begin to wonder if it's true. Aren't they idealizing their spiritual master, trying to present him as a picture of perfection? Rather, their spiritual master might have been "rascal number one," as Prabhupāda puts it. He might have been more like Vālmīki before he met his spiritual master. It's nothing to be ashamed of.

I would like to tell you frankly how I feel about capturing the examples in my own life of less than perfection. I feel a sense of accomplishment when I can take a piece of the mosaic of my life and place it in the context of my present. I feel that sense of accomplishment especially when I take a shattered piece, a painful piece, a piece that had no connection to Kṛṣṇa consciousness. Of course, there is no shortage of such memories, and by letting them out one by one and then leaving them behind, I almost feel as if I am paving the way to the more pleasant memory that Prabhupāda saved me and that my life now is real.

# Bay Terrace

Bay Terrace is one of the stops on the Staten Island Rapid Transit (SIRT) toward the south. Although I'm sure things have changed since I rode the train in the 1950s, the route is probably similar. The train began at St. George and traveled south toward the smaller towns and countryside until it reached the end of its line and turned north again.

I still remember looking at the scenery from the metal-screened windows. The train had hard, straw-thatched seats. They were probably plastic or fiberglass, but they looked like rattan chairs with crosswise stitching. Some of the chairs could be reversed, and at the end of the route, the conductor would walk down the aisle and swing them all around to face the other direction.

I lived in Great Kills, which although not one of the smallest towns, was still quite small. Going south the train stopped at New Dorp and then a few more towns after that, then a tiny town called Bay Terrace, which was right before Great Kills. Bay Terrace was so small that the conductor would walk through the cars (the trains were often no more than two or three cars long), asking if anyone planned to get off at Bay Terrace. If not, he would speed right through it, provided there was no one waiting on the platform to board the train. Bay Terrace was the sticks.

Why does Bay Terrace come to mind? It just popped into my memory today and with it, the name of the first girl I ever dated. Her name was Alice Erickson. When I was about eleven or twelve, we went to a square dance together. By today's standards, dating in those days was backward. The schools were strict and the young people were not promiscuous. I didn't know anyone who took drugs. We had never even heard of marijuana. Alice Erickson was in my class. I don't remember much about her except that she was bigger than I was—I was quite skinny—and that she invited me, probably by phone, to a dance.

Alice was a kind of no-account person. To this day I don't know why she asked *me* to go, but it was thrilling to go to a dance with a girl. My parents were agreeable—in fact, they drove me to the dance—and it was at night! I hardly ever went out at night beyond my own yard or neighborhood.

I'm embarrassed by the antiqueness of this memory. Imagine talking to a person of the '90s about square dancing or the fox-trot. Did we wear plaid shirts? Was there a fiddler? A caller?

Neither of us had hit puberty yet. I still remember standing on the floor like pieces on a checkerboard and the caller telling us how to dance: curtsy to the left, bow to the right. First go forward and then go back, then in and out. We were weaving and maneuvering around, sometimes dancing away from our partners and sometimes joining them again. Sometimes we would link arms at the elbow and sometimes swing each other by the hand. Our spirits were high and our faces flushed. We were happy to get through the steps with the music.

It was otherwise an uneventful evening. We didn't end up hating each other when the evening got too long and I didn't step all over her feet. I counted it as a triumph—I survived my first date. We didn't follow it up by becoming friends. I never asked her out after that and she didn't invite me to any more dances. I still don't know why she invited me in the first place, but somehow my name came up and she reached out.

# Nail-biter

I used to bite my fingernails, even after I became a devotee. In the fourth grade, the teacher would examine our fingers every week just to see if we bit our fingernails. I wasn't the only one who did it, and that's why she would inspect everyone's hands. Everyone accepted it as a bad habit. If she found a nail-biter, she would put red Mercurochrome on his or her fingers. It was like being branded with the scarlet letter. Actually it was worse, because if you then put your fingers into your mouth to bite your nails, the taste was horrendous. We'd have to wait until the Mercurochrome wore off.

When Hayagrīva wrote a pamphlet to teach the BTG editors grammar, he wrote this in a sample sentence: "When a person takes to Kṛṣṇa consciousness, he stops all bad habits, such as biting his nails." I remember feeling sensitive to his choice of examples, although his only motive was to explain a point in grammatical composition. I couldn't understand why, although I had taken to Kṛṣṇa consciousness, I had not stopped that habit.

Another time I was distributing BTGs on the Boston Common. This was at a time when the Boston Common was filled with hippies day and night. I would go from group to group to sell our small stash of magazines, and at one point I approached a group and made my pitch. One of the girls spoke frankly: "How come you bite your fingernails?" Here I was, telling them about Kṛṣṇa and everything, and she asks me a question like that. I replied that I wasn't perfect, not a pure devotee. One of the other members of the group appreciated my response, "That's cool. You know, that's all right, man."

Because I was hurt by the exchange, I later confided my feelings about it to another devotee. He defended me: "How dare they say that to you? You're on the spiritual platform. They don't know your transcendental emotions. If you bite your nails, it's for spiritual reasons, not because you are not Kṛṣṇa conscious." Oh well.

I once discussed it with Jayādvaita Mahārāja too. We were in Madison, Wisconsin at the time. One day by chance he looked at my fingers and saw that for some reason, two of my fingernails were long (the others were all bitten down). I must not have had time to work on them yet. He said, "Oh, you are keeping two of your nails long?" He thought I had a reason for it—maybe it made it easier to play the *mṛdaṅga*. Then I confessed, "I'm a nail-biter. This is my shame."

I did get control over it for awhile, but it would always come back to me, an unwanted habit. I did it when I felt anxious. One devotee said that nail-biting was meditating on dead matter.

When I was young, I was told by a young girl that a person who bites their nails eventually has to have their stomach cut open to get out all the little bits of nails they have swallowed. I was young enough to half-believe it and it scared me; it sounded so scientific. All those little bits of nails don't get digested, but they gather and gather until they fill up part of your stomach. Then you have to be operated upon to remove them. Oh my God!

Of course, I learned to recognize other nail-biters. Some of them chew right down to the quick. These were usually the poor kids who didn't hide their nail-biting. I was more presentable; I would only do it in private. I even thought it looked disgusting. To this day, I still think it's a pitiful habit, especially in an adult. It must be the sign of bad nerves. I no longer bite my nails, but I do pick at the skin around my cuticles, and since I've become more philosophical and insightful, I have an explanation for it now. My explanation is that I express my sense of mortality by doing this. Although I pretend I'm not going to die by busying myself with so many activities, the fact is all these activities will be destroyed at death. This is one subconscious way I remind myself of this fact. It's a kind of nervous reaction or expression of anxiety. Prabhupāda says the birds show anxiety, even when they're eating, by looking around every few seconds, but humans tend to avoid the anxiety of approaching death and eat and sleep and watch television as if they hadn't a care in the world. Somehow I have come to see my nail-biting or cuticle-picking as a recognition that I'm going to die and that I should feel the anxiety that such a remembrance produces. Therefore, I'm sympathetic to the nail-biters out there. It's a difficult habit to cure, but I suppose, as Hayagrīva wrote in his pamphlet on grammar, "When a person takes to Kṛṣṇa consciousness, he gives up bad habits, such as nail-biting."

Well, he doesn't always. He may take to Kṛṣṇa consciousness and keep a few bad habits. *Api cet su-durācāro bhajate mām ananya-bhāk.* We don't think him less of a devotee for his bad habits, but trust that they will go away in time. The main criterion by which to judge him is whether or not he is devoted to Kṛṣṇa. It could be that he is a saint, but a nail-biter. As a saint, his anxiety may be over the fear that he has not attained love for Kṛṣṇa, and perhaps he bites his nails out of that anxiety. Who knows?

# Father

Whenever I read Śrīla Prabhupāda's dedication to his father in the *Kṛṣṇa* book, I am touched.

> To my father, Gour Mohan De, 1849–1930, a pure devotee of Kṛṣṇa, who raised me as a Kṛṣṇa conscious child from the beginning of my life. In my boyhood ages he instructed me how to play the *mṛdaṅga*. He gave me Rādhā-Kṛṣṇa Vigraha to worship, and he gave me Jagannātha-ratha to duly observe the festival as my childhood play. He was kind to me, and I imbibed from him the ideas later on solidified by my spiritual master, the eternal father.

What a fortune it is to have a Kṛṣṇa conscious father, a father who loves you enough to give you spiritual life, a father who knows how to love you at all. My childhood was not filled with the loving care of Bengali Vaiṣṇava family life; rather, I was lonely. Instead of my father directing me in *pūjā*, he left me to play baseball alone in the yard.

My father would occasionally play catch with me. I have an early memory of him playing catch out on the street with me in Queens. He had a pipe in his mouth. I threw the ball high and as he backed up and reached to catch it, he suddenly hit against a telephone pole and almost dropped his pipe. It was an awkward moment—my heroic father had somehow been compromised. I was still young enough to see my father as young and handsome and faultless. It wasn't until we moved to Staten

Island that I began to see the chips in his armor and that I became sullen and less responsive to him.

The biggest difficulty I experienced with him as I grew older was that my nature was so different from his. He simply couldn't understand me, and he tried to squelch what was natural in me and create someone more according to his own definition of a son. This was the real tragedy in my relationship with him. He didn't leave me any room to be who I was. When I was five and he was away at war, he sent me boxing gloves. When he came home, and as I grew up, I saw that he was a right-winger and that he valued everything America stood for. He had worked hard to be part of the American dream. I was a poet, an artist, a left-winger. I was everything he wasn't.

Yet I suppose he loved me in his own way, even if he didn't understand or approve of me. I wanted to be a college professor, but my father thought that was the "end of the line." It was a non-career in his eyes. Rather, he encouraged me to become a Naval officer. I signed myself into the Naval Reserve officer training program when I was seventeen. My father had assured me that I would be drafted when I was eighteen, and before that happened I could choose something better than the Army, which he considered third-class. I was so naive and gullible and uncreative in my thinking at that time—still willing to follow his lead—that it didn't occur to me that I could have avoided the military altogether just by following my dream to become a professor. Students didn't get drafted.

On our way home, on the night when I signed into the Navy, my father and I sat in the car in the dark. As he shifted gears he asked, "Is this really what you want?" It was such a strange question to ask at that point and I still wonder why he asked it. Maybe he thought I was a little *too* malleable. Maybe it worried him. But I wasn't able to stand up for myself yet. That came later.

When I think about it now, I feel sorry about what I suffered in the Navy. I feel tender toward my young self, and I realize that my father probably meant no harm. He simply didn't know my heart, my soul. I became a rebel and then I met Prabhupāda and my life changed forever.

If I were to write a dedication to my father, this is what I would write:

To Stephen John Guarino, a pure devotee of the school of hard knocks, who raised me to be a good *mleccha karmī* from the beginning of my life. In my boyhood he gave me boxing gloves and did not teach me to worship God, but pushed me into the Navy. He spurned my attempts to become an intellectual and mocked my sensitive nature, and when I met my eternal spiritual master, he rejected me completely. Nevertheless, he was such a physically strong man, simple and courageous, that I imbibed from him an impression of masculine strength, which I can use in my attempt to become an unflinching devotee of the Lord. This teaching has been solidified by my spiritual master, the eternal father.

# Our Memories, Our Truths

Sometimes we think our memories are either too mundane, too painful, or too self-serving and self-centered. Or perhaps they are too gossipy, even when they are devotional remembrances. Admittedly, those are dangers. I would like to contend that although some memories may have those defects, they are also a life, our life. We're protagonists in a drama—not the be-all and end-all, and usually not even the heroes—just tiny parts of a history. We don't know any other story as well as we know our own. Napoleon—or even the past *ācāryas*—are distant figures from the past; what we know now is the streets in which we grew up, the *saṅkīrtana* that we did, the bits of our past that tell our own truth.

Fortunately our truth coincides with the preaching orbit of His Divine Grace A. C. Bhaktivedanta Swami Prabhupāda. He lifted us up and therefore we remember him. By his grace, we have done some preaching ourselves. Even *our* lives have become worthy of remembrance.

And what of the memories that are not connected to Prabhupāda? Well, all we can do is to see them as entities to be brought to Kṛṣṇa consciousness. We can preach to them, or we can drop them just as we drop attachments that are no longer relevant to us. It's not that recalling our past will itself make us think only of

Kṛṣṇa, but perhaps such recall will help us to understand that the worthy memories are the Kṛṣṇa conscious ones. We'll become more grateful for them. All those memories we gathered before we came to Kṛṣṇa consciousness—we can let them go. They are not really part of us any longer. We can only see that old life in Kṛṣṇa conscious terms.

But what if we can't let them go? What if we feel them too strongly? What if they cry out for acknowledgment?

Then we should acknowledge them. We don't have to indulge in them to acknowledge them. Rather, we can hope to find Kṛṣṇa in such memories in a form yet undiscovered. He is the life of our lives; it is He who makes our memories vivid and vital. Yes, the pain we suffered in the past is an obvious sign of our lack of Kṛṣṇa consciousness, but we will still allow ourselves to remember and feel it, to feel the injustice, the anger or whatever. They are real enough to drag us to Kṛṣṇa's lotus feet.

# Emotion Evoked by Jazz: Is It Always *Māyā,* or Something Else?

Coltrane, my old friend, master musician, you were wrong. I know that now. You were playing the same old riff. You gave yourself to it, but at what cost? I listened to you when you slowed down and assured me that a love supreme does exist. I know now who that is, that He is beyond black and white, beyond hate, beyond those smoky nightclubs, the tight-lipped embouchure, Elvin Jones' drumsticks clashing, McCoy Tyner on keyboard, and me an outcast from them and outcast from all that father and mother bred me for. I worked hard to buy your albums, Coltrane, because you allowed yourself to chant "a love supreme"—your black voice raised in a sing-song chant.

When a practicing devotee asks the inevitable question: "What does this have to do with Kṛṣṇa consciousness?" there are different ways to answer. We can be stern: "It has *nothing* to do with Kṛṣṇa consciousness. It is *māyā* and should therefore not be discussed." Or we can answer in another way: "Exactly. What *does* this have to do with Kṛṣṇa consciousness?" Does the music have an inner form? Does it sing of an incoherent expression of love of God? That very question—"What does this have to do with Kṛṣṇa consciousness?"—can become a search and a cry.

# When To Fight

We used to go on *harināma* on the Boston Common, especially on weekends, when there were hundreds of young people lounging on the lawns there. Some of them were homeless and slept on the lawns. This is 1968–69, before we had our more established spot just outside the Boston Common by the subway stop. We used to chant right up on the grass. The crowds used to close in on us and listen, but it was always tense because there were always some rowdies and hecklers. Our *harināmas* became almost like lion-taming acts as we tried to give enough energy to the chanting to hold the rowdies off for awhile. We were usually successful; the *kīrtana* generated such energy that we couldn't hear the heckling much and the rowdies somehow didn't dare to break through the invisible ring of the holy name to attack us. The most they would do was mock-dance or hurl insults. It would get even tenser, however, when we stopped the *kīrtana* for a few minutes to make a speech. We even wrote to Prabhupāda about it. He told us not to bother making a speech, but to go on chanting if that was the situation.

One time a group of Hell's Angels came by and broke up our chanting. They were much more inimical than the usual rowdies and hecklers. There was only a small group of devotees on the Common that day—Pradyumna and I and maybe a couple of other young men, such as Devānanda and a boy named Patita-pāvana. Jadurāṇī was also there with two other women.

At first the Hell's Angels were loitering in another part of the park, but I was aware of them. The Boston Common is not such a large park that we wouldn't be aware of people coming and going. As soon as I saw them, I became afraid that they would come down and do something to us. I knew they would have the power to break through that invisible circle we had drawn around ourselves. Sure enough, they did just that after we had been chanting for awhile. I don't remember how many of them there were.

Just as we wear our uniform *dhotīs* and *sārīs*, so the Hell's Angels have their uniforms—unshaven faces, heavy bodies, and sleeveless denim or leather jackets with Hell's Angels emblems on their backs. They came and watched what we were doing, then they interfered. Someone forcibly took the *karatālas* out of my hand and wrapped them around my neck. Once the music stopped we were powerless. Then they took the drum from someone else and yelled, "Stop! Stop this!"

Of course, the people didn't support us; they just watched. I was the leader of the devotees and I had several choices: we could fight, resist them in some other way, go on chanting somehow or other, or acquiesce. I decided to acquiesce; I accepted that our public *kīrtana* was over. Rather than open ourselves to the possibility of violence, we decided to leave. That's all we wanted to do.

I do remember one painful moment: as we were leaving, a few people came up to us and said sympathetically, "It's just terrible that they did this to you," but then I looked back quickly and saw Pradyumna talking to one of the gang members. He had a friendly expression on his face, trying to win them over and to prove to them that we were not weird and that we didn't need to be enemies. As he was talking, another Hell's Angels gang member got on his hands and knees behind Pradyumna. Then the first man pushed Pradyumna backwards and he fell over the second man's back. I was pained to see them mock his attempt at human empathy. It made him look like a fool.

We were sobered by the experience, and as we drove back to the temple, we discussed whether it was right that we had retreated. Later I wrote a letter unburdening myself to Brahmānanda, who was at that time still the temple president in New York. Brahmānanda was built like a football player. I had no doubt that he would have acted differently in such a situation. I also described in my letter that chanting with us that day had been a follower of an impersonalist yogi, a Western man, but he had taken the attitude that everything was one and that we should be nonviolent and accepting regardless of what happens to us.

Brahmānanda replied, "How were you different from that guy? You didn't fight either." Then he described a fight that had broken out recently just outside the New York temple storefront with some local rowdies. When the rowdies saw how enthusiastic the devotees were to fight, one of them yelled out, "Hey, leave them alone. They're religious," meaning that we were probably so fanatical that we would fight to the death for our principles. His letter was a reprimand.

I felt as if I had been a coward. Then Jadurāṇī wrote to Prabhupāda and asked if we should try to kill the demons. She also thought we should have fought. In the meantime, I began to build my resolve to face off with these hoodlums the next weekend when we took our chanting party out.

The next Sunday we went to the Common and I brought something that would serve both as a musical instrument and as a weapon. Actually, it wasn't much of a musical instrument—it was two large pieces of metal that I would slap together. It didn't make much of a sound. I psyched myself up that I would hit the hoodlums with these pieces of metal if they approached us again. I began to allow anger to build in me and think of the confrontation to come as a matter of life and death.

From our chanting spot, I could see the Hell's Angels in the park. I felt like I was walking through town in a "High Noon" movie, waiting for the shoot-out. As the crowd pressed around us, a rowdy, not a gang member, lobbed an empty bottle in at us and it hit me on the head. It didn't break, but it hurt and stunned me. A few people nearby expressed sympathy, but no one did anything. I continued to slam those pieces of metal together waiting for the moment of truth. It never came.

Of course, our determination to chant in public was always being tested in this way. And Prabhupāda did respond to Jadurāṇī's letter: "Killing proposal is not good. We have to kill them with arguments and reason—not with sticks and weapons. Jadurani—I am very glad that you want to kill the nondevotees. You should, however, leave the matter to your good God-brothers who will take care of it. I am pleased to learn of your spirit of protest, but sometimes we have to tolerate."

# The Past Leaks Into The Present

I would like to say something more about that "Hell's Angels" story. That story has its merits as a story—it has adventure, danger, a good theme (courage), conflict, and a devotional resolution. I told it without trying to make myself a hero. The only problem is that I didn't discover anything about myself by telling it.

Simply telling stories of my life is not the purpose behind this book. I am looking for "epiphanies," peak moments of awareness in my life as I have lived it. Perhaps it's too ambitious to expect to find an epiphany in every remembrance.

Then what? Am I writing a memoir? I don't want to become an old-timer reliving his life from an easy chair, even if the stories are adventurous. But why not? One memoirist, Patricia Hampl, says, "Refuse to write your life and you have no life." It's not enough to tell a story from your life; you have to reflect on it and consider its meaning. The memoirist has to listen attentively to his own story as he tells it. Hampl's point is that our first remembrance of a particular incident might be falsified. We may have already defended it and then accepted the defense as part of the story. If we listen attentively, however, we will separate out truth from falsity and allow the images of the incident to touch upon the hidden emotions the story evokes. In this way, we will be able to tell a story that is more faithful to the inner self. Then we'll get the "epiphany" we are looking for.

Patricia Hampl goes on to defend the memoirist. She says that she doesn't agree with the opinion that autobiographical writing is done only by self-absorbed people:

> True memoir is written in an attempt to find not only a self but a world. . . . Actually, it begins as a hunger for *a* world, one gone or lost, effaced by time or a more sudden brutality. But in the act of remembering, the personal environment expands, resonates beyond itself, beyond its "subject," into the endless and tragic recollection that is history.

We have a more simple and direct route to connect, not with the "tragic recollection that is history," but with the Absolute Truth. Does remembrance of the past help us achieve the Absolute Truth? It can help, although it is not, of course, the Absolute Truth in itself.

Let's try to follow Ms. Hampl's method. I just told the story about how the Hell's Angels disrupted our *kīrtana*. According to Hampl, we have different memories stored from the innumerable things that have happened to us. It's explicable why we choose one and not another when we are asked to tell a story. There must be something in the particular remembrance that is important to us, but we don't always see it on the first telling. If we think about what it is that gives energy to the particular story, however, we may find a clue.

Just now, thinking over that story, I find that the greatest "energy" or emotion came not from the part about the Hell's Angels, but from what my wife said to me: that it was weakhearted not to fight with the Hell's Angels and that the next time we have a problem with them, we should be prepared to fight. She said it as a stern truth-teller, but not necessarily as my closest friend. Her words did make me face myself, however: could I measure up to what she deemed brave and right?

As I stood by the skylight early this morning remembering this, I suddenly remembered, almost with surprise, that I will die. My memories are a search for coherence. As the past leaks through me, they return me to the present.

# Epiphanies

I don't have a dictionary with me but I recall that "epiphany" means a moment of special insight. It may appear to be a coincidence, such as when we overhear strangers speaking and they suddenly say something relevant to our lives, or it may come as a memory that enlightens us about something in a present situation we are facing. In his *Confessions*, St. Augustine says that it was an epiphany that brought about his conversion to Christianity; James Joyce also uses the word to explain the special moments of insight he experienced when writing.

Rūpa Gosvāmī experienced an epiphany when he was still a minister for the Nawab. On one rainy night, the Nawab called for him on an emergency errand. As Rūpa Gosvāmī traveled through the downpour, he passed a washerman's hut. The washerman heard Rūpa Gosvāmī's palanquin pass and said, "Who could be out on such a terrible night?" His wife answered, "The only people who would go out on a night like this are the dogs, thieves, or slaves of the king." Her words hit Rūpa Gosvāmī and he realized that it was true, he was a slave of the Nawab. He immediately decided to renounce his connection to the king no matter what the price. Bilvamaṅgala Ṭhākura had a similar realization when the prostitute Cintāmaṇi said, "If you had as much affection for Kṛṣṇa as you have for me, you would be a great devotee."

Whatever epiphanies I remember from before I met Prabhupāda tend to be sentimental. Once I was visiting a few hip friends on the Lower East Side. They were playing a record of the Thelonius Monk Quartet, which featured Monk's rendition of "I'm Getting Sentimental Over You." I suddenly saw the essence of our Lower East Side vision and it moved and touched me. The music was sad and sweet and I felt love stir in me and then overwhelm me. I still remember the feeling I had while listening to that music, although I was never able to recapture it.

I also remember a year or two later cooking in the Boston storefront's improvised kitchen and getting an epiphany. It suddenly occurred to me that all my life I had had a feeling that I was special, that I had a special destiny, and that that destiny was being fulfilled by my becoming a devotee of Kṛṣṇa. Meeting Prabhupāda and surrendering to his order was the actual fulfillment of all my desires, all my feelings of cherishing the sacred, of all the things I had thought but never expressed to my parents or anyone else. That special destiny was summed up by my standing in a little improvised kitchen in Boston cooking cereal for my Godbrothers and Godsisters.

# Blackberry Picking

When I was a boy living at 125 Katan Avenue in our little Cape Cod house, we sometimes went blackberry picking at a place you could reach by walking down Katan Avenue and up a hill that had no housing development on it. There was a small wood there, although it was more like an overgrown field of brush and weeds and plenty of blackberry bushes. I would bring my mother's aluminum pots and pick and pick and pick. My fingers would be stained from the juice and pricked by the thorns until the whole bucket was filled and brought home to my mother. Those were happy days.

Someone once said that Thoreau had such good intelligence that he should be managing the nation, not managing a group to pick blackberries. Thoreau preferred to stay out of politics, though, and I can attest that blackberry picking is good fun.

I also read a poem once describing the suffering conditions the writer experienced on his rounds as a male nurse in a hospital ward. In the midst of his poem, he suddenly tells of a character in a Chekhov story who says he has achieved happiness because he was finally able to grow gooseberries on his own land. Another character in the story laments that people who think like this are suffocating the world. How can they possibly be happy amid so much suffering? Shouldn't we all be doing something to alleviate world suffering?

In Kṛṣṇa consciousness we pick blackberries and offer them to Kṛṣṇa. Just to see the devotees honoring them as the Lord's *prasādam* is wonderful. That's Kṛṣṇa conscious community life and it can alleviate the world's misery because Kṛṣṇa is in the center and His mercy is available to anyone who will take it. We can't all be militant peacemakers as this poet suggests we become. We can't just go out and spread the teachings, give out books, and call our duty complete. To be effective and to attract people, we need recreation, agriculture, and cow protection—culture. As long as we live in this world, we should take the opportunity to pick blackberries, and we shouldn't be ashamed of our juice-stained fingers as if they prove we should be doing more.

# Spring Potpourri

I remember stepping outside Matsya-avatāra Prabhu's house with him and his saying that May is the best month because it's neither too hot nor too cool. Trees bloomed in his yard over the neoclassical statues he has placed here and there, and I found I agreed with him. It was nice to think that I could do something with that feeling: I could come back another May.

Then he and I and his son sat together while his wife and mother and daughter served *prasādam* from the kitchen. He has a nice painting of Śrīla Prabhupāda on the wall, an original, rather small; it has a triptych effect because on either side are two doors that can be closed over the picture.

The different places we visit have a kind of finality to them, especially ones we won't visit again. Even places like Matsya-avatāra's house where we will go again won't be the same forever. I won't always be able to sit at his table with him and enjoy the *prasādam* his mother has prepared and go out the door together to decide that May is the best season. Things will change despite our attempts to remain stable and fixed. "Time I am, the great destroyer of the worlds."

During another spring we arrived at the German farm and a small group of devotees came forward to meet us. Their *kīrtana* was soft. I didn't recognize Aṣṭaratha Prabhu among them, or Kṛṣṇa-kṣetra Prabhu either, because I didn't know them well and they were such unassuming *brahmacārīs*. How I have come to like their company.

Of course, I remember our late spring visit to Cozzile. We drove the winding roads up out of the city one year and arrived on an Ekādaśī. Śrīdāmā and his wife were waiting for us at the house, the front door open. It was dusk and they served us Ekādaśī biscuits and milk. I ate with pleasure in a room upstairs. It was a strange room with a high bed and pictures of Christ's crucifixion and one of Mary. The room was dark, but I could feel my readiness to write there. Nine days later, I had completed *From Imperfection, Purity Will Come About*. What I didn't write of it in that room, I wrote while sitting outside at a shaky white patio table under the cherry trees.

After that, I really struggled with free-writing and came out with a book called *What Shall I Write?* It's half sunk in the sand now—it was never published—but I like the fact that I struggled so much and tested the writing process. At the end of it, I discovered the numbered writing session, something just my own.

I also took walks with Śrīdāmā in Cozzile. It was a happy time, although it has now become tinged with sadness because Śrīdāmā has left me.

# Spiritual Aspirations

The Lord told Brahmā to tell the demigods that their wives (*sura-striyaḥ*) should take birth in the families of cowherd people in Vṛndāvana. Thus they would have the privilege of joining in Kṛṣṇa's pastimes. Śrīla Prabhupāda explains that if we are pure devotees at the end of our lives, we will take birth in the universe where Kṛṣṇa is currently exhibiting His eternal *līlā* and be trained for service in Goloka Vṛndāvana.

Do you remember that teaching?

Oh, yes.

Well, here it is again, right in the early verses of the Tenth Canto. It's not something to debate or doubt. The material scientists can't understand it, and we are also free to accept it or not.

When will *we* be able to join Kṛṣṇa's pastimes? We have to want it very badly, greedily, transcendentally. It takes lifetimes of devotional service. Better, therefore, to move along and not hang back doubting whether Kṛṣṇa even exists or asking questions like, "How is it possible?" We are filled with Western material prejudice and that is our misfortune.

I remember hearing Prabhupāda tell us about this training we would receive. I also remember joking about it in the *saṅkīrtana* van on the way to the Boston Common. Līlāvatī said she would like to go back to Goloka Vṛndāvana for a feast or two with Kṛṣṇa, play with Him awhile, and then return to this world to preach on

His behalf. We'd heard that the highest aspiration of a devotee was to preach in Lord Caitanya's movement in this world. We had heard it was even better than desiring to stay in Goloka. How superficial was our understanding! Our choice was not between staying in Goloka (as if that were within our grasp) and being a perpetual preaching-traveler, a Nārada Muni. Our choice was between practicing *vaidhi-bhakti* and falling back into the material pool. *Māyā* was not completely convinced that we wanted no more part of the material world, and she was always ready to test us to see whether we had actually come to disturb Kṛṣṇa. If we are disruptive to the society of devotees in this world, how can we ever expect to fit in to the harmony of the spiritual world?

Still, the philosophy is there. If we become pure in this lifetime, we can go to be with Kṛṣṇa somewhere in the material manifestation in our next life.

Lord Brahmā told the demigods that Saṅkarṣaṇa would appear first as Kṛṣṇa's older brother, Balarāma. Yogamāyā or Viṣṇumāyā, the Lord's potency, would also appear and bewilder persons like Kaṁsa into thinking he could kill Kṛṣṇa. (That's Mahāmāyā. Visnumāyā would act as Yogamāyā and make Yaśodā and other intimate servants of the Lord think that they are His mother or friend or lover.)

In this way, Lord Brahmā pacified Mother Earth by assuring her that Kṛṣṇa would remove the burden she felt from the demons.

Does this news pacify me? Are my doubts and fears dispelled? I would like to respond as Arjuna did at the end of the *Bhagavad-gītā:* "Yes, my Lord, my illusion is now gone. I am unafraid and prepared to act on Your order. I accept all that You have said. You are the Supreme Personality of Godhead."

I remember hearing about Kṛṣṇa from the Swami and concluding, "He is the most relishable form of God." Kṛṣṇa is the best. Even then it began to dawn on me that He wasn't a myth or the God of the Hindus, and I began to have faith that this Vraja boy could be all that they say He is and all that He says He is. *Mattaḥ par-ataraṁ nānyat:* "O conqueror of wealth, there is no truth superior to Me. Everything rests upon Me, as pearls are strung on a thread." (Bg. 7.7)

# An Act Of Faith

Madhu is ill. He lies in bed with his hand on his head. Praghoṣa is supposed to bring him some homeopathic medicine tonight, the only medicine he is willing to take. I feel for him and I'll certainly be relieved when he gets better. I ask hopefully, "Feeling some relief?" He looks brighter and says, "Yes. My stomach has relaxed and my headache is gone." Until he gets better, I can't get close to him. He doesn't want me to read to him and I don't ask him to fulfill his secretarial duties. There's nothing much I can do for him. I just go upstairs and continue my program. He'll be all right in a day or two.

On my way out for another session in the shed, I saw that Madhu was at least sitting up now. He told me that he had been unable to chant any rounds yesterday. I assured him that it was all right and that he could make the rounds up in the future. Then he said that he had chanted five silent rounds today so far. With a pained look on his face, he added, "How will I think of Kṛṣṇa at the time of death if I can't even chant a few rounds when I'm sick?" It was a stark remark. Here I was, feeling chipper in my sweatshirt, my bookbag hanging from my shoulder and pen and paper in hand, ready to go out to the shack for some late morning work. Maybe what he is experiencing now is as bad as it will get at the time of death. Then it occurred to me how when people are ill, they live in a different reality from those who are not. They don't want to be cheered; if you try to cheer them, you will be left holding the bag of your own false optimism.

I shook free of his gloom and continued out the door. He'll be better in a day or two. I have to find my memories—as if it's important.

It *is* important. It is an act of faith. We are what we were. We who live in a Kṛṣṇa conscious continuum need to see our lives—our entire lives—from a Kṛṣṇa conscious perspective. Don't live on the surface.

# Competition Among Godbrothers

I remember the competition among Godbrothers. I was involved in it and now I'm relieved to be free. One Godbrother said that actually, we were competing to do something big to catch Prabhupāda's attention. We all wanted to have a project that he would recognize. We weren't content to just do our service peacefully; we wanted to be outstanding.

Prabhupāda recognized and even incited our "transcendental" competition. He noted one year that Jayatīrtha's zone had sold more books than Tamāl Krishna Mahārāja's zone. He said, "Tamāl Krishna will have a heart attack!" But it was difficult and heavy to always be competing, and I want to admit that now.

I think of devotees like Rāmeśvara Swami and how they influenced me and drove me to collect more money for the BBT. Even after Prabhupāda's disappearance, when the zonal *ācāryas* began to lead the movement, the competition continued unabated. There was no question of my being a quiet person who did what I wanted or even what I could; I had to strive to keep up with them.

When Prabhupāda visited the Manhattan temple in 1976, I often didn't get to ride in the car with him because I wasn't one of the four or five persons who could fit in the car. When he went for a one-day visit to Gītā-nāgarī, I could have squeezed into the bus, but I just didn't want to. Instead, I stayed back in New York and felt separation in my room while I read his books. Actually, I preferred it, although I certainly still felt connected to him. During that same visit in 1976, the library party—myself, Mahābuddhi, Ghanaśyāma—told Prabhupāda that we had now covered America and we wanted to go to Europe. Prabhupāda's smile came spontaneously and made us happy. I wasn't estranged or alienated from him, but I had to keep a certain distance. Getting close meant having to deal with all those secretaries and world leaders, and it was too much for me.

I felt the same when I visited Prabhupāda during his last months in Vṛndāvana in 1977. I was there when Prabhupāda decided to make his last visit to the West. Tamāl Krishna Mahārāja was his secretary and Gurukṛpa was there, and I felt out of place. At the same time, I wanted to be with Prabhupāda. When Prabhupāda decided to go to England, I decided not to accompany him. It's not that I could have spent time with him anyway; I might have seen him for a few minutes here or a few seconds there because I had no secretarial services to perform.

And why didn't I? Because my relationship with Prabhupāda was so much in awe and reverence that I couldn't cross the barrier and take him in my arms as they were doing. Of course, I massaged him and offered other bodily services, but there was a barrier I just couldn't cross. Part of it was my own selfishness: I wanted my own space, I wanted my own schedule, my own life. To be his servant in those last months meant being constantly on call. I might have been able to do it, but no one asked me to do it, and neither could I have lived with those who were performing that service.

This memory began focused on the relief I feel of not having to compete with my Godbrothers anymore and has led me to examine something about the nature of my relationship with Prabhupāda.

# Memory As Political

In her essay, "Memory and Creativity," Patricia Hampl writes that one important reason to tell your own story is to correct mistaken versions of history. Memoirs must be written, she says, because we each have created our own version of the past and we must live with our version and its inevitable subjectivity. She says that if people are not willing to speak their truths, then whole histories can be rewritten.

> As Czeslaw Milosz said in his 1980 Nobel Prize lecture, the number of books published that seek to deny the existence of the Nazi death camps now exceeds one hundred.
>
> What is remembered is what *becomes* reality. If we "forget" Auschwitz, if we "forget" My Lai, what then do we remember? And what is the purpose of our remembering? If we think of memory naively, as a simple story, logged like a documentary in the archive of the mind, we miss its beauty but also its function. The beauty of memory rests in its talent for rendering detail, for paying homage to the senses, its capacity to love the particles of life, the richness and idiosyncrasy of our existence. The function of memory, on the other hand, is intensely personal and surprisingly political.

We all have our histories and few of them are so personal that they do not involve others. For example, I remember how years ago, I became the sole initiating guru for huge population areas: New York City, Northeast U.S., the Caribbean, Ireland, Vancouver, etc. Those who are reading this account after the fact and who don't know the history shouldn't think that being a guru was a trip I was taking on all on my own; it was the ISKCON system. Still, I have a certain amount of responsibility for what happened during the zonal *ācārya* years. It's hard to take responsibility. I prefer to remember myself as a law-abiding ISKCON citizen, a gentle fellow who went along with the crowd, who wanted to do the right thing, but it can't end there. Actually, I should have seen the higher principle at work and transcended institutional policy and risen to a higher level of morality. That was too difficult for me to do at the time. My inability had such a deep effect on so many people as well as on myself that there is nothing left for me now but to live as I am living—not quite as ready to fall into line with policy that although fully endorsed, may be faulty.

The whole story is sensational. It is also steeped in institutional politics. I'm not even sure why I started telling this memory. Perhaps to give an example of how when you go down certain avenues you meet too many monsters. And of course to show that my version—anyone's version—is relative.

To be honest, I now feel deceived by the invitations of the temple presidents, but I was vulnerable and willing to quickly assume the role of guru. I want to admit that now and to understand how neither I nor the devotees who invited me were absolutely right or absolutely wrong. I know that the temple presidents wanted to protect their turf from too much control. They were the real authorities there and needed the ISKCON figurehead guru to endorse their domains.

A lot of people liked me in those days. I was in a top position and I was malleable. They could remain the real leaders and I would be the figurehead for them. It's not that I was completely naive to this, but it would have taken more strength and purity than I had to find the balance between the flow of the institution and my own nature.

This type of memoir sounds a little like the kind of memoirs told by ex-presidents. I have never read any of them, but I can imagine, for example, Jimmy Carter's version of why the American hostages could not be freed from Iran. He would describe himself as having done the best he could in an impossible situation, and his version would contradict the picture we have of him as a weak and ineffectual leader. Ronald Reagan certainly played on Carter's weakness in order to defeat him in the election. We all want to set the record right by telling our own side of the story.

I discussed some of my zonal guru experiences in *Litany For the Gone*. I confessed that I had wronged some people during the zonal *ācārya* days by allowing them to come under the control of people who were under my authority but who didn't take care of them. In fact, I still think my biggest defect in those days was that I accepted the role of guru but heard only second-hand reports of a person's progress. These reports were not always accurate.

After *Litany* was published, a devotee I mentioned in the book wrote a letter full of loving anger. She said that I had actually only admitted to the tip of the iceberg. She didn't feel I had seen my actual wrong. She then described her version—how I stood by while she was manipulated and mistreated by the leaders under my authority. Her letter was stinging, yet I could see that she hadn't written out of maliciousness but only to set the record straight from her point of view. I felt chastened by her words, and felt that she had written the more truthful account.

After saying all this, I realize that the one danger in everyone writing their personal remembrances is that we may fall into bitter debates about what actually happened, especially if our intention in the telling is to make ourselves look right and others wrong. If we could express our wrongs openly and be willing to admit both to mistakes and subjectivity, then maybe we could find peace. Is that possible?

# Garden Seat

I'm sitting in Uddhava's backyard in Wicklow, on a white bench in the "Prabhupāda garden." The bench has a cupola-shaped structure over it which is made of coated metal. It invites creepers to grow on it, and some flowering vines have obliged. I'm facing the Pride of India tree—now a two-foot sapling—and the many other flowers. Beyond this garden, I can see Uddhava's vegetable gardens under the poly tunnels. In my attic room here, it's so peaceful that I can sleep without wearing earplugs. All I hear is the water filling the toilet tank downstairs. If I use my imagination, I can dream that it's not a toilet tank, but a country creek.

Right now, the only sound intruding is of some big, motorized vehicle in the woods. I don't know what it is—maybe a farmer cutting hay on a tractor—but it sounds as if some beast of a motor is about to roll out of the trees and into this garden. I'll try to keep it at bay while I think.

I'm at somewhat of a crossroads right now. I just finished writing a book called *Pada-yātrā*, where I took an imaginary two-week walk with my pen. Since then, I have done six days of hardworking writing sessions. Then I started getting headaches while working on them, and since the headaches made the writing sessions become more diffuse, I became exhausted by writing them and decided to find something gentler to do.

I have been taking morning walks and coming back to write poems. This morning I read one poet whose poems were as stark as the newspapers. He was writing about Bosnia. He told about a child being crucified and a soldier who was hung, and there were descriptions of suicide and child abuse and other horrors. He said, "We're all in this together."

Are we? I wonder. Here I am, sitting on a white bench in a peaceful garden trying to find a few minutes of silence, and it's not that I am unaware of people's suffering out there. I know that even while sitting among the bell heather and lord's candles and fan palms that there is no ideal state anywhere in the material world.

The poet-hermit, Robert Lax, admitted in an interview that while living in his hermitage on the Greek island of Patmos, he sometimes listens to the news over the BBC. The interviewer asked Lax if he felt any sense of moral duty "to be informed of all the disasters you can do nothing about?" Here is Lax's reply, which I think is pertinent to what I have been discussing here:

> If a man is working on the discovery of penicillin, I think he is right to keep on with his work even if all the cities in the world are falling. He should keep to that work. We'll need some penicillin. I don't think you can rush off with a gun on your shoulder every time there's an alarm. I think if there's destruction and turmoil in the world, people need penicillin. They need any good thing you can produce.
>
> —From *Hermits, The Insights of Solitude*

Anyway, I'm not going to feel guilty that I am here and not in Bosnia. Rather, I hope that if I describe my life in Kṛṣṇa consciousness as honestly as I can and offer it to Kṛṣṇa and the devotees, I will be of some help to those who are suffering. Does that sound presumptuous? Maybe. It will all be resolved by time.

# Pain

I can't imagine the severe pain people who have cancer must suffer. What about Thérèse of Liseux? She refused to take morphine, but instead offered her pain to Jesus, who himself suffered for everyone's sins. She told her sister Céline that whenever she expressed her pain, Céline should say, "Good." They had an intimate relationship and Therese did not always keep up a good front before her sister; she sometimes cried from the pain. Her sister refused to say "good," and the dialogue went like this:

Thérèse: It hurts.

Céline: No.

Thérèse: It hurts.

Céline: No.

Thérèse: It hurts.

Céline: Good.

Thérèse: It hurts good.

Suddenly Thérèse said that she had no more pain.

Saints suffer, and ordinary people do too, and they sometimes cry out from their hospital beds. In material life, we sedate them so often that they spend their time unconscious, spared from the pain. In Kṛṣṇa consciousness, however, we recognize that pain provides a lesson in detachment. Therefore, we pray to Kṛṣṇa for the intelligence to surrender to Him through our pain.

It's difficult not to seek pain relief. In my case, at fifty-seven, I am at a productive age. Men are elected President at my age. Although the body may be in decline, the brain is agile and experienced. I won't be elected President, but I do want to write as much as possible. That's why it's so frustrating to be knocked out of service by pain for a week, my duties stolen from me. That's one reason devotees don't like to simply surrender to the pain as Thérèse did, without trying to alleviate it: we want to be active in devotional service. We also need the vigor to chant our *japa* every day in good consciousness. It's hard to put out the energy when you're in pain.

Many devotees have experience in living with pain. Before I had regular pain, I used to wonder what kind of cross I would have to bear in this life. I even thought that if I had to choose, I would prefer physical pain over problems with others because all the difficulty would be contained within my own body. It seems my wish was granted. Anyway, it's a common cross.

I remember one time years ago the pain was intense behind my eye. I lay down on the couch at the BTG house, and although devotees tried to help me, the pain remained sharp. In fact, it was then that it began to become a regular occurrence and I would simply have to lie down until it passed. Gradually, I began to let go of my expectations. I couldn't fulfill big writing quotas—I could write only three or four pages a day—and I could not continue my regular duties. We have to be prepared to scale down our activities and accept what comes, although it is natural to resist the decrease until we are sure we are dying.

Pain is something of the material realm. Kṛṣṇa does not feel pain in His spiritual body, and when we have spiritual bodies, we won't either. When we are liberated, we will be so absorbed in thinking of Kṛṣṇa on the spiritual plane that we won't even feel the material pains that come from fasting and whatever other austerities we perform. Sanātana Gosvāmī didn't feel the pain of his blistered feet as he walked on the hot beach, and Haridāsa Ṭhākura was spared the pain of being caned in twenty-two marketplaces. I'm not there yet. If I try to ignore headache pain and push on with duties despite it, the pain intensifies and I am forced to stop. For me, pushing on is a kind of self-imposed physical abuse. A more advanced devotee may be able to transcend the pain, but it's not something we can necessarily imitate. The important point is not to become absorbed in pain relief. We have to remain philosophical. When Swami Satcidananda visited Prabhupāda in the hospital in 1967, Prabhupāda, as if explaining his illness, said, "It's *prakṛti*." They were speaking Hindi, but this much I understood as Prabhupāda shrugged and gestured to his body.

I had some insight when I was forced to live at Gītā-nāgarī as an invalid during the spring and summer of 1985. I came to understand that pain is a true, physical state, not a temporary aberration from health. Rather, health is the temporary and illusory state. I learned to expect more and more pain as my body aged and especially at death. How is it possible for death *not* to be painful? Therefore, living with this pain was training me to live through that pain. My suffering wasn't a waste of time. If at the first sign of pain I am not able to remember Kṛṣṇa, then I have not learned the lesson.

I also learned that service doesn't have to be full of activity to be active. It can be subdued. It may be reduced to consciousness, where even in the pain-filled state, we simply maintain an abiding faith and love, which we offer to Kṛṣṇa.

# Remembering The Divine Spark To Preach

Memories are as rich as loam. I remember one time after the GBC meetings in Māyāpur, some of us were in New Delhi together. We had rented two rooms in an inexpensive hotel. Rūpānuga Prabhu was there, and Balavanta Prabhu. We all felt a nice sense of dutifulness after the meetings and we were eager to return to the West. I think this was in 1975.

I especially remember Rūpānuga discussing how we should be preachers. We were all based in temples, so he said that when people come to the temple, we should be anxious to go forward and speak to them about Kṛṣṇa. We shouldn't get bogged down behind our desks as temple administrators. The real life of Kṛṣṇa consciousness —the secret of existence itself—was this great gift Prabhupāda had given us to preach to whomever we met.

We all wanted to do it. Rūpānuga gave a crude analogy: just as a prostitute eyes a man and thinks how to entice him as a client, so we should look upon people as prospective candidates for Kṛṣṇa consciousness. I also remember Balavanta's enthusiasm.

Those particular men would really stress whatever they were into. So many of my Godbrothers were like that—Bhagavān, Rāmeśvara—strong men. When they felt that something should be done, they not only felt it personally, but advocated it for the whole society. In this case, I felt the thrill of Rūpānuga's words and the happiness we all felt of having our own turf in the U.S.A. in which we could preach. It felt so good to be going back after our *yajña* in India, not to some material family, but to the field Prabhupāda had given us.

The inspiration of this meeting was that they were talking about it as if it were a new discovery. Maybe by our enthusing each other and then keeping in touch we could devise different preaching strategies. We made plans, although it basically came down to a personal sense of being alive as devotees, as preachers, and a readiness to follow Lord Caitanya's order to the Kūrma Brāhmaṇa: *yāre dekha, tāre kaha 'kṛṣṇa'-upadeśa*, be ready to talk to anyone and be inspired to influence that person to become Kṛṣṇa conscious. That is the way of divine life.

I don't know if our inspiration continued to run high when we got back to our temples and faced our lack of daring, our lack of compassion, and the paperwork on our desks, but the longer we stayed in Prabhupāda's movement the more we wanted to preach. No one, of course, has ever really been able to preach as he did, or to have the patience he had to gradually find conditioned souls and bring them to Kṛṣṇa consciousness.

# Father and Prabhupāda

I have a mental image of Steve Guarino, my father, standing outside the storefront at 26 Second Avenue and waiting for me. I can't remember exactly why he was there—it doesn't fit in with some of the chronology of my becoming one of Swamijī's followers—but I do remember that once I had met Swamijī and taken to the practice of Kṛṣṇa consciousness, I called my parents on the phone and told them about it. That's when they told me they would have nothing more to do with me if I pursued Kṛṣṇa consciousness. I told Prabhupāda about the conversation and that seemed to be the end of my relationship with them outside of a few more phone calls.

Somewhere in that history, my father and I made arrangements to meet and spend a few hours on Manhattan's Lower East Side. I think we even went to a nearby Italian restaurant for dinner.

I don't remember so clearly what happened. I just remember walking south on Second Avenue toward the storefront and seeing my father standing outside, waiting for me. He was about five foot seven and he was in good shape, although he weighed about 200 pounds. He was a stocky man, rugged-looking, a man who prided himself for his strength and courage. He was wearing a fedora, which, although conservative, had a sporty touch—maybe a colored feather. I can't remember if it was summer or winter. If it was winter, he would have been wearing a hip-length car coat, and if it was summer, he would have come in a suit jacket without a tie.

All I can remember is the mild sense of shock I felt that he actually came. It was such a strange juxtaposition to see him at the storefront. I was already twenty-six years old and firmly established in who I was. Meeting with my father didn't have the same power to shake me as it had in the past. I had already weathered most of those storms, at least on the conscious level, years earlier and followed my hip life despite their protest. I doubt they were even aware how much I was indulging in LSD and marijuana. Suddenly, I was following Swami Bhaktivedanta, and although they were opposed to that too, I was an adult, a case worker in the Welfare department, old enough to do my own thing. Were we trying to make peace at this meeting?

My father said that he had been invited into the storefront by one of the devotees, but he had told them he preferred to wait outside. He didn't say this critically; he sounded amused and friendly.

It's strange that that's all I remember about this meeting. I guess it's not much of a memory, but it was the last time I saw him. It was 1966. Only last year, 1995, did I learn while reading a letter from a friend that my father had died of a heart attack in Philadelphia in 1987 at the age of seventy-eight.

This shred of memory intrigues me because it feels like a juxtaposition of my father with Śrīla Prabhupāda. Where was Prabhupāda when my father visited? Was he upstairs?

# We Have Changed For The Better

I remember being in a college classroom after giving a philosophical presentation. The professor said that although the class appreciated my talk, the philosophy was abstract to them. They would like to hear something practical, such as how living the philosophy had made me a better person. I accepted his challenge and told the class that I was happier, less distressed mentally, etc. That's a change that's hard to describe, but it's an important change. It means we shift from egocentric to even a somewhat Kṛṣṇa-centric person, and our hearts are lightened.

This is certainly true in my life, and to this day I feel the power of that shift in consciousness. I remember mentioning this either to my Uncle Sal or my Aunt Mary when I was explaining to them why I had become a devotee. I had little contact with my parents or relatives after I joined, so this was a rare conversation. It took place over the phone. I wanted them to know that I was not only normal, but that I was benefiting from Kṛṣṇa consciousness. I told them how self-centered I used to be and how much less self-centered I was now. Perhaps it was too subtle for them to understand, but I thought they would remember how I was and notice the difference.

I guess a similar shift might take place if someone stopped living an ordinary life of sense gratification and dedicated himself to an altruistic cause. He would become more generous, more big-hearted. That's how I felt. I knew it was Kṛṣṇa consciousness that was making me more modest and humble and that the false ego attitude was something I no longer wanted. I didn't even want to become aware of how great a shift I had made. I was afraid it would hurt my humility. I didn't want to be proud of holiness. Even today it's not something I wish to measure and offer as scientific proof of the efficacy of Kṛṣṇa consciousness. I know many devotees have had the same experience.

I recall riding in the van back to a campground for the night after an evening preaching program at a university. We did this program a number of times, so I can't remember a particular evening—we might have been at the University of California's campus in San Diego or at a person's home in Santa Cruz. Perhaps it wasn't much of a program—only a dozen people—but we would have done what we had gone there to do: chant Hare Kṛṣṇa, speak on the *Bhagavad-gītā*, distribute *prasādam*, and probably collect a small donation. On the way back, we would have exchanged stories about how the people were favorable or indifferent and we would have felt satisfied with our lives. Just to return to a campground instead of a home and a grind in the city made us feel even happier and more dedicated. And of course we didn't know it then, but part of our happiness was that we were young.

That's something we have to look at—the power of youth to propel us toward happiness. It's not uncommon for older devotees to remember their earlier days in the movement as happy and to feel that they have since become stagnant. We have to constantly prove to ourselves that this is not true. Therefore, we have to qualify what it means to feel advanced or to be happy in Kṛṣṇa consciousness. Were we more Kṛṣṇa conscious when we were absorbed in Prabhupāda's order to preach and physically capable of carrying it out without any consideration? Or was that service, although valid, external and busy and not necessarily better than what we are doing today? We have to face that question.

If it's true, as they say, that we are what we were, then we should string together as many Kṛṣṇa conscious activities and thoughts as we can so that they will weigh us in as devotees at the end. It may not be possible to prove to the nondevotees that we are significantly better for practicing Kṛṣṇa consciousness, but we know the truth of what we were and what we are and can judge for ourselves. The nondevotees judge everything against their own standard of happiness: sex, money, and other material achievements. But it's between us and Kṛṣṇa. We measure everything by Kṛṣṇa's estimation. As Prabhupāda said, we want to get a certificate from Kṛṣṇa that "This person has pleased Me. " No other applause is necessary or even wanted.

# Joie De Vivre

What is the place of *joie de vivre* in Kṛṣṇa consciousness, especially for a neophyte devotee? We tend to be afraid of expressing love for life, and we're almost certain that it's sense gratification. Are we afraid to admit that we are happy to be alive?

Of course, we are convinced that the only purpose of life is to serve and please Adhokṣaja, the transcendental Lord who is beyond all sensual perception, and we know that only fools and rascals are interested in serving matter. What joy is there other than the joy of serving guru and Kṛṣṇa? We even suspect *that* joy as if it were a materially motivated pleasure. Devotees suffer from a searing introspection on this point and tend to be hard on themselves. (The material psychologists are almost the antithesis of the devotees. They encourage people to grab all the gusto they can get.)

I am asking this question as I face my life in *Memories*. Why is it I am remembering things that happened before I became a devotee? I want to contact my sense of being alive. Is it wrong, or is it honest?

As we grow older both in body and in Kṛṣṇa consciousness, we tend to perform our spiritual duties mechanically. It's a kind of deadness. We have to feel. It's important. That doesn't mean we don't have the responsibility to center our feelings on Kṛṣṇa, but to do that, we may have to start at any feeling without worrying whether or not it's qualified to be called spiritual. We have to trust ourselves that much.

We have lived through things that we liked and things that we didn't like. We can leave them in the past or face them as they strike us now, at this moment. Our memories and our present activities can have meaning if we allow them to. For example, last January I decided to wear only *khādī*. I thought it would enhance my humility because as a guru and a *sannyāsī*, I could choose silk or a finer grade of cotton and thus distinguish myself from an ordinary *brahmacārī*. Of course, it's a ridiculous proposition, but nevertheless it's my little attempt and I derive pleasure from making it, knowing what *khādī* has come to mean to me.

Similarly, once in a while I like to be in a place where I can take a walk in the morning. I wear sweat pants and boots when I walk—I step out of uniform. Perhaps this is not the strictest observance of my *sannyāsa* vows, but it's a small concession, a pleasure, and I guess I will just have to make such concessions until I learn to find all my pleasure in Kṛṣṇa.

Kṛṣṇa consciousness shouldn't be dry *vairāgya*. Prabhupāda told me that when I mentioned that we had bought a better motorhome for traveling. He told us to be comfortable so that we could be strong and happy to practice Kṛṣṇa consciousness. This is a dynamic of serving in a spiritual movement in the material world.

# "But Trailing Clouds Of Glory . . . From God Who Is Our Home"

That's a line from Wordsworth's "Ode: Intimations of Immortality from Recollections of Early Childhood." He says that the child is born "Not in entire forgetfulness,/ And not in utter nakedness,/ But trailing clouds of glory do we come,/ From God who is our home." Then he describes the prison walls that slowly close around the boy as he grows, which means that although we are born in an almost divine and natural state, we are gradually socialized and lose touch with the spirituality and beauty of our environment. Occasionally the poet has intimations of such beauty again, especially if he lives close to nature and gives himself time to reflect on what he sees. For most people, however, it is simply lost. Related to this is the concept that real experience is derived through the senses; the more intellectual we become, the further from real life.

Of course, a devotee doesn't agree with either of these statements. We think of the great *gosvāmīs*—Rūpa Gosvāmī, Sanātana Gosvāmī, Raghunātha Bhaṭṭa Gosvāmī, Lokanātha Gosvāmī—and how the older they grew, the more glorious they became. Raghunātha Bhaṭṭa was a wonderful child. He sat on Lord Caitanya's lap as a boy of eight, but his life did not end with that one experience. As a young man he visited Lord Caitanya and was blessed by His embrace and a gift of the Lord's *kaṇṭī-mālā*. On another visit to Nīlācala, the Lord presented him with His *tulasī-mālā*, which he then wore around his neck in Vṛndāvana while he recited *Śrīmad-Bhāgavatam*.

After Lord Caitanya's disappearance, the Gosvāmīs grew more and more intense in their feelings of separation and entered *līlā-smaraṇam* to a degree that they never did in their youth. It's not that their study or even their age dulled their senses and drew them away from reality. Rather, it was just the opposite. They were free in youth from the usual vices associated with the senses—sex desire, bodily identification, intoxication with the world, strength, and physical beauty—and they became more and more concentrated on the spiritual world.

# Places

Hare Kṛṣṇa dāsī wrote and asked, "You always seem appreciative of the places where you feel the atmosphere is conducive for your service. Are there any places from your childhood (or any time before you met Prabhupāda) that you would like to visit in the expectation that they might be good places to chant or write?"

She then told me of two places she would like to visit from her own life. One was a salt marsh in Lancashire, England where her grandparents used to live. She described how the road would be covered twice a day by the tide and how bleak and deserted it was there. She said she found both her parents and grandparents "coarse and gross beyond belief," so she would spend hours walking the mud-flats. The other place was at the university she attended in a coastal village in Wales. In the winter, the beach was deserted, and she would walk it alone. "If only I had had a beadbag! At night you could walk along the beach. Because the sea and wet sand were reflecting the same dark blue as the sky, it was like walking into the sky."

They sound like good places to walk and chant. I can think of one place, although it's not a place to chant. That is, I think of walking the deck of the USS Saratoga when the ship was in port. Of course, we weren't able to do that when the ship was at sea because the USS Saratoga was an aircraft carrier. We could only walk the gang-walks and passages along the edge of the ship, and even that was forbidden when the planes were taking off and landing. When the ship was docked, however, especially in the U.S., we could walk across the entire deck. I walked it and can remember the loneliness I felt as I thought of the authors I was reading—Kierkegaard, Kafka, and others. It evokes something in me, but I wouldn't want to return to that ship deck, and neither could I do any service there.

A few years ago I stopped by my home in the village of Great Kills, Staten Island. It felt odd to see it again after so many years, because of course, it wasn't the same Staten Island of my childhood. It was like walking in a dream while everyone else was awake.

I suppose I could go back to such a place to preach. I know devotees who do that—return to their childhood home with their reputation of success in the world, and use that reputation to preach Kṛṣṇa consciousness. I once considered writing another Nimāi story in this vein. Nimāi would open a preaching center in Great Kills and preach to someone who would resemble my teenaged self. The story's conflict was in "my" parents' objection and the reaction of the people in Great Kills. I thought my story could deal with some anti-cult issues. My character would be writing a paper for school about the cults, so his first visit to the center would be purely academic. I'm reluctant to write fiction, though, so I never wrote that story.

To be honest, I don't think Great Kills would be the best place to establish a preaching center. Better to do it in Manhattan or Brooklyn. But there are other places that might work too.

I grew up in Queens, but it's so congested now, and so degraded, that there is nothing left to return to if you are looking for solitude. Even when I was a kid, my mother and I returned to Queens to reminisce, but local kids shot peas at us with peashooters.

I traveled as a sailor and visited many Mediterranean cities—I even went to Greece and Istanbul—but I saw only the insides of sailors' dives. Why would I want to go back to those cities? No, it seems that all the best places are those I have discovered since I have been a devotee.

I have plenty of memories of places from the last thirty years. They almost feel like neighborhoods. Most people don't have the opportunity to travel that I have, and they think of a neighborhood as something familiar and limited. I think of the many rooms and streets and places to walk that resemble one another all over the world and see the link between them all whether they are in Guyana, Trinidad, Ireland, India, Italy, France, Spain, or America.

Ultimately, the whole world is open if what we want is a little peace and interest to hear from Prabhupāda—open beyond the Navy bunk, the four walls of any house, the beach in Wales or the salt marsh in England, the mountains in many places. We can reach the milk ocean and beyond to Vṛndāvana-dhāma from any place. That is Prabhupāda's gift to us.

# Perpetual Motion

Where will this end? I keep wearing out sweatshirts and getting new ones, and new dictaphones and slippers and knit hats. There is no end to the pen refills, and a new book is always coming out. I'm always sharpening new pencils. Things go on year after year—to India and back and to India and back. I live as if the world is never going to end its perpetual motion.

But this scene is not perpetual. This elderly *sannyāsī* and his little life dramas, his headaches, Madhu and the van—they are all part of an identity with variations on the theme. It will come to an end.

Incidents pop into my memory: sitting in the Boston University library reading Prabhupāda's books before they were published, editing. I see myself absorbed in the *Śrīmad-Bhāgavatam's* philosophy. It drew me in and carried me away from the outside world.

Then standing with Śāradīya after we had been presented with an honorarium at Boston University. She told me how she had learned to smile by practice—a woman's secret way to charm strangers.

Then singing in night clubs with the devotees. I don't want to dwell on all these memories. They make me restless, they're so skimpy. All I want is to bow down to Prabhupāda and say, "Please accept me. Please forgive me. Please give me Kṛṣṇa consciousness and good service engagement. I do remember you and here I am in the present wanting to engage in your service."

All those mantras I've chanted, do I remember them? All those times I uttered Hare Kṛṣṇa. Agrāṇī Prabhu taught me how to breathe out so I could chant five mantras on the exhalation. When your breath runs out, you inhale quickly and chant five more as you slowly let your breath out again. He said I could speed up my chanting in that way. We chanted sixty-four rounds together in Vṛndāvana for awhile. Mahākrama was there too. I think of those devotees and it's painful to remember how we have all gone our different ways. I wonder what will happen to me. Where will my memories finally end?

This life is just a "spot journey," as Prabhupāda calls it, and we're moving onward toward our goal. We may not reach it with these memories and this body. Mundane memoirists dwell on this life as the all-in-all, although some have a vague idea that they are drawing from Jung's collective unconscious or from some other cauldron of memories connected with the Union of Man. That's how they define memory, that it's not something personal to the individual, but it's a vast pot of impressions from which we all can draw. They theorize and remember their mundane experiences and explore their outer world, but they don't remember God. They think the outer world is inconceivable, but the inner world is more inconceivable because memory, knowledge, and forgetfulness come from Kṛṣṇa. And who can understand that?

Real remembrance, therefore, is Kṛṣṇa conscious memory, "*smaraṇam.*" *Smaraṇam* means we remember Kṛṣṇa's form, name, pastimes, and entourage. That keeps leading me back to the same question. In my other personal writings I say I want to speak perfect philosophy but that I can't always keep my mind on it.

Therefore, I free-write about what my gut tells me as I read *Bhāgavatam* or the nature of the struggle to drag the mind back verse after verse. Similarly, *smaraṇam* means thinking of *kṛṣṇa-līlā*, but at this point, I can't always keep my mind on Kṛṣṇa's pastimes but find some other memory welling up in me. How do I fit them into my Kṛṣṇa conscious life? And the truth is, I find real *līlā-smaraṇam* impossible. Rūpa and Sanātana Gosvāmīs lived in constant *līlā-smaraṇam* and were emerged in Kṛṣṇa's Vṛndāvana pastimes. Because their minds were in Goloka Vṛndāvana so much of the time, their bodies were completely neglected. They lived in trance. If by chance they lost their ability to engage in *līlā-smaraṇam*, they would try by any means to recover that ability. They were *rāgātmikā* devotees. I am not. If I were to report only my remembrance of Kṛṣṇa's pastimes, the report would cover only a tiny portion of my day, a tiny percentage of my actual consciousness or experience. How could I possibly hide the big lumps of dirt under the carpet? And it's not *all* dirt, either. There are also all my attempts to become a devotee and to deal with the reality of who I am. I try to "Kṛṣṇa-ize" my memories and to make peace with them. I know that my perpetual motion is actually temporary and that some of my memories have no absolute value or standing, but I still have to admit my actual level and go forward from there. In that sense, remembrance is an item of *sādhana*, even if it's not *līlā-smaraṇam*.

# Who Cooked For Kṛṣṇa And Kṛṣṇa's Devotees

Allen Ginsberg began his poem "Howl" by starting every sentence with the word "who." Then he would list one after another in a Whitmanesque way a variety of Beat generation exploits. Just by starting each sentence off with one word, memories can be listed in stanzas. Hayagrīva dāsa borrowed Ginsberg's devise and wrote a poem about Prabhupāda: who came to America without any money to spread Kṛṣṇa consciousness, who conquered the psychedelic mind, who preached in this way or that, etc.

I don't think I'll use that particular device, but I would like to give a flow of pictures and experiences of things I know have happened in ISKCON over the years. I'm also going to try not to be apologetic about it. Share the truth.

I remember cooking on Janmāṣṭamī. I have very few ISKCON cooking experiences. I did cook the Sunday feast in Boston sometimes and I was happy to do it. Even now when I remember it, I can still see the cauliflower and potatoes in their creamy yogurt sauce. It seems all I needed were good ingredients and it was bound to come out successful. I used to like to cook *halavā*. I preferred to make it out of wheat germ with plenty of butter. I even made *gulābjāmuns*. I was cooking *gulābjāmuns* one Saturday night while some teenage hoodlums threatened us. At times like that, I kept cooking to stay sane.

I also used to cook breakfast when I lived in Boston. I remember putting a lot of powdered milk into the porridge and comparing notes with Advaita dāsa, who cooked the breakfast for the devotees in New York. We called our porridge "heavenly" because of a phrase we had read in the *Rāmāyaṇa* about porridges with magic properties that could make women pregnant and grant other boons. I would always put powdered milk in mine, and of course sugar. I usually cooked Quaker Oats and I remember the delight I felt in seeing it all come together and then adding fruit toward the end. It was a meal in itself. Of course, we offered the porridge to Kṛṣṇa, but my main meditation was to make it as delicious as possible for the devotees' pleasure. We were so young we could get away with a lot—we could eat a lot, laugh a lot, and depend on Kṛṣṇa's mercy.

As time went on, however, and especially as the Boston temple grew, I took on more administrative duties and others cooked. I have cooked only rarely since that time, except when I entered the kitchen on Janmāṣṭamī to cook for the Deities. Gradually, I have grown out of touch even with that.

Of course, I had to cook for Prabhupāda in 1974. That was a challenge! I gradually learned to cook to his standard, but it was a struggle. I was never what you would call a good cook. When one meal didn't turn out well at all, Śrutakīrti arrived at the last moment with some *samosās* his wife had made and Prabhupāda really liked them. I felt saved that at least Prabhupāda had been offered something good for lunch. Prabhupāda came out into the little room I used as the servant's quarters to show me how to make instant sweet rice, how to make *capāti* dough with more liquid to make it come out right. He personally showed me how to make a few things, but I didn't really have a kitchen—there was no water in the room and I had only one electric burner. I remember taking a pot off the burner and putting it straight on the floor. When I picked up the pot again, a round piece of linoleum came up with it and there was a circle missing from the floor.

After I left Prabhupāda's personal service, I again lost touch with cooking. I didn't roll up my sleeves in any kitchen. Gradually, I lost my confidence in the kitchen and I didn't dare to do it anymore, even when I thought of it. I know I have missed out on the special nectar of mixing with devotees and working against the clock. I can see from my distance how exciting it is to prepare the Lord's plate and carry it onto the altar, cooking and praying to Kṛṣṇa to make it come out right, cooking huge quantities to satisfy the devotees. Maybe this year on Janmāṣṭamī I'll go and make *halavā* for Kṛṣṇa. After all, this is a "kitchen religion"; the skills we learn here may be useful even in the spiritual world.

# At The Time Of Death, Will You Remember As Prabhupāda Remembered?

I remember the white powder we rubbed on Prabhupāda to keep him cool in April 1977 and throughout the summer months. I don't know if it relieved him in any way, but he said his mother used to pat it on him. We patted it all over his body.

When Prabhupāda said he didn't want to live anymore and some of the GBCs and intimate servants left his room to discuss it, I stayed for a little while in his room patting his feet with that white powder. I felt resigned that he would leave. Everything else was just a kind of painful delay because the conclusion felt so inevitable. I still remember that white powder. Was it talcum powder? Baby powder? Will someone put that on my body at the end and will it remind me of Prabhupāda? Will it give me courage?

Prabhupāda said that nothing should be artificial. We want our experiences to flow from the heart. For example, imagine trying to pretend that you're noble and composed and ready to die, or pretend that you're interested in preaching right up until the end, so you tell one disciple to go to Moscow with a theater troupe and another to go to Bangladesh with the courage of a British soldier and the kindness of a Bengali mother.

You give each disciple some last instruction by which they can live out their lives. But it may not be like that. Perhaps you'll have no energy at all to divert to others. The pain may be intense—much worse than you expect—but if you have faith in your identity as Kṛṣṇa's servant, then you will find that clear space that awaits the faithful devotee, and that will be the natural condition.

Of course, I am not dying today. Therefore, I still need to spend time researching the Absolute Truth. As Prabhupāda said in a lecture in Vṛndāvana, those who are pure and simple will accept Kṛṣṇa's words straight from the *Bhagavad-gītā*. Kṛṣṇa says that He is the cause of everything (*vāsudeva sarvam iti*). If we doubt His words, then there is nothing left for us to do but to do the research to prove Kṛṣṇa's claim. Prabhupāda doesn't denigrate that research; rather, he encourages us to take it up in whatever work we are doing. If we are cooks, we cook, and if we are writers, we write, but we should look for Kṛṣṇa behind everything, as the source of everything, and we should do it before we die.

# Re-reading The Early Chapters Of Kṛṣṇa Book As We Approach Janmāṣṭamī

I just finished reading the chapter, "Prayers by the Demigods for Lord Kṛṣṇa in the Womb." One important function of the memory is to recall what we have read. One way to retain the information is to repeat it to another devotee soon after we have read it. Even in mundane education, they say that material is usually retained until the exam, and then the degree of retention falls sharply the less the student uses the material. We have to use what we hear in the *śāstra*. Somehow, we have to be sure that it makes an impression on our minds. If what we are reading seems vague or irrelevant, then we will never remember it.

In this chapter, Prabhupāda refers to the verse, *samāśritā ye pada-pallava-plavaṁ*, "For one who has accepted the boat of the lotus feet of the Lord, who is the shelter of the cosmic manifestation and is famous as Murāri, or the enemy of the Mura demon, the ocean of the material world is like the water contained in a calf's hoof-print. His goal is *paraṁ padam*, or Vaikuṇṭha, the place where there are no material miseries, not the place where there is danger at every step."

This chapter also contains the verse, *ye 'nye 'ravindākṣa vimukta-māninas*, "O lotus-eyed Lord, although nondevotees who accept severe austerities and penances to achieve the highest position may think themselves liberated, their intelligence is impure. They fall down from their position of imagined superiority because they have no regard for Your lotus feet." Prabhupāda quoted this verse to prove that we can know Kṛṣṇa only by His mercy. In the *Kṛṣṇa* book, Prabhupāda tells us that the Lord's appearance is the answer to all speculative iconography about the nature of God, and he says that knowledge of Kṛṣṇa given in the scripture and passed down to us by Lord Brahmā is *vijñāna*, realized knowledge. I have been quoting these verses and purports for years because they are some of my favorites.

I remember repeating one of them once and feeling as if I had really grasped the point. I even added my own footnote to it when I spoke (I was lecturing to a college class). My realization was simple: there is theoretical knowledge and there is realized knowledge. If theoretical knowledge of God is not enough, how do we become realized? We become realized by hearing from those who are realized, someone like Lord Brahmā, and then accepting what they say thoroughly and openly. We don't become realized by performing extra *tapasya* or by having mystical experiences. We simply have to be submissive and open to someone who possesses realized knowledge. Of course, that means we have to believe that there *are* persons with such knowledge, but *vijñāna* means to faithfully accept and repeat what we have heard from authority.

We used to be so innocent in our following of Prabhupāda, and in those early days in Boston, we would repeat what Prabhupāda taught. A learned devotee was someone who had memorized large sections of Prabhupāda's books and who could repeat them during a lecture. I remember feeling annoyed sometimes when I thought the devotee was parroting Prabhupāda and not speaking from his own realization. Nevertheless, the ability to repeat Prabhupāda verbatim is a virtue.

I also repeated what Prabhupāda had written and I still do. Once I was invited to serve as the head *pūjārī* during a Deity installation in Mexico City. I lived in Dallas at that time, so although I preferred not to travel, I couldn't refuse this request because it was so close. Anyway, during the lecture I spoke about how people describe God and how they tend to speculate on what He looks like. When God says He is the oldest, they picture Him as an old man. If God should appear, however, then we will no longer have to speculate. The truth will be evident.

As I remembered this today, it reminded me of something that took place while I was still in the Navy. There was one sailor in the PIO office who was an artist. He took advantage of the ship being docked in Italy and our being on liberty to go to Rome to see the Sistine Chapel. Michelangelo's painting of God is what most people imagine God to be like: patrician, muscular, bearded, and very old. He rides on the clouds and reaches His finger out to create by His divine touch. This sailor (I think his name was Paul), whose job it was to paint accurate renditions of jet planes and other military equipment, expressed sadness that the paintings in the Sistine Chapel were falling apart; they would eventually be lost to the world.

I told him I thought it was good that they would be destroyed. He was shocked. My Lower East Side friends had made me an iconoclast. I liked to shock people. I also thought we should face our mortality. I told Paul that art should not maintain the illusion that we will live forever, that our culture will live forever. The old works should be destroyed and replaced with works of contemporary expression. Paul was scandalized.

These thoughts before Janmāṣṭamī while I look for my *vijñāna*. Sometimes we repeat without the freshness of realization, but we can taste these pastimes as new each time we open the *Kṛṣṇa* book. The demigods conclude that Kṛṣṇa comes to the world not to kill the demons—that has already been done by His energies—but just to enjoy with His devotees. Devakī should not worry; Kṛṣṇa will protect her. The demons will be killed. The demigods then return to their own planets and we are ready for the next chapter, "The Birth of Lord Kṛṣṇa."

# Valuing Memories As An Act Of Kṛṣṇa Consciousness

One of the most remarkable things about memory is how much we actually forget. I seem to retain only abstract remnants, shreds of what actually happened. Words provide the medium to rescue even the shreds, and they often empty the store. Why do we speak our memories, then? Because they summon up feelings.

For example, when I met with Śrīla Prabhupāda in his room before I went to Boston on his behalf, I admitted to him that I felt intimidated by the mission. He told me to sound off the big cannon of Hare Kṛṣṇa. His words encouraged me; they made me feel brave. He was on his way to India to recover his health at that time (summer of 1967) and I didn't know if he would ever return, but he was sending me as his missionary son to open an ISKCON center in Boston.

In farewell I prostrated myself before him and then felt his hand rubbing up and down on my back several times. It was a wonderful blessing. It was a physical exchange, but I felt more physical happiness from the touch of his hand than I had ever felt in any other attempts I had made to feel physical gratification. His touch was completely transcendental. After I had gone back downstairs, I excitedly told the devotees about it, but ultimately it was mine, for me and no one else. It gave me the strength to carry on in Boston during the years when it was tough and I felt alone, and even when Beantown threw at me all it could in terms of gang members and indifference. Such was the potency of his hand on my back.

That memory is genuine, and perhaps by hearing it, it will evoke emotion in you as it evokes emotion in me, or at least some understanding of how the spiritual master's touch can generate inspiration in the disciple. But it seems like I should do more with this memory than just *feel* it. I should honor it in some way. That's where we often become mechanical. If we worship a *mūrti* only by reciting mantras, we don't really seem to honor him as real and true. If we neglect our memories, it's just another part of our overall thoughtlessness. When Lord Caitanya, expressing the mood of the *gopīs*, remembered the wonderful times He had spent with Kṛṣṇa, He said that if He ever got such an opportunity to be with Kṛṣṇa again, He would worship the minutes and hours of that union by offering incense to the passage of time. *Līlā-smaraṇam* includes worship.

How do we honor our memories? The residents of Vṛndāvana *lived* on their memories after Kṛṣṇa went to Mathurā. When Uddhava came to Vṛndāvana, Nanda and Yaśodā asked him if Kṛṣṇa remembered His mother and father and the *gopīs*. Did He sometimes ask for them? When Kṛṣṇa met the residents of Vṛndāvana at Kurukṣetra during the solar eclipse, He assured them that He did think of them and remember them always. The Lord and the devotee always remember and never forget one another.

# "My Trade And My Art Is Living"— In Kṛṣṇa Consciousness

This morning I suddenly remembered that my mother used to wash my hair in the kitchen sink. It was a once-a-week ritual, and we both enjoyed it. I don't know why I didn't wash my own hair—this memory is not one from infancy but from young childhood when I was certainly old enough to take a shower on my own—but it was the source of another loving exchange between mother and son.

Remembering this made me wonder at its significance. Michel de Montaigne, the famous sixteenth century autobiographical essayist, wrote in defense of memoir, "My trade and my art is living." Montaigne wrote various precepts for writing about the self and about using memory to arrive at the closest approximation of ourselves of which we are capable. He doesn't consider it an act of ego to describe the self because "No particular quality will make a man proud who balances it against the many weaknesses and imperfections that are also in him, and, in the end, against the nullity of man's estate." In other words, facing death is crucial to any honest self-assessment.

Here are some quotable remarks by Montaigne:

> What I write here is not my teaching, but my study; it is not a lesson for others, but for me.

And yet it should not be held against me if I publish what I write. What is useful to me may also by accident be useful to another.

Custom has made speaking of oneself a vice, and obstinately forbids it out of hatred for the boasting that seems always to accompany it. . . . I believe that the rule against speaking of oneself applies only to the vulgar form of this failing. . . . What does Socrates treat of more fully than himself? To what does he lead his disciples' conversation more often than to talk about themselves, not about the lesson of their book, but about the essence and movement of their soul? We speak our thoughts religiously to God, and to our confessor, as our neighbors do to the whole people. But, someone will answer, we speak only our self-accusations. Then we speak everything: for our very virtue is faulty and fit for repentance.

I hold that a man should be cautious in making an estimate of himself, and equally conscientious in testifying about himself—whether he rates himself high or low makes no difference. If I seemed to myself good and wise or nearly so, I would shout it out at the top of my voice. To say less of yourself than is true is stupidity, not modesty. To pay yourself less than you are worth is cowardice and pusillanimity, according to Aristotle.

Coming back to my little self, I am looking at these memories that have made an impression on me. If I try to claim that they are philosophical or wise or religious, I will be guilty of pretension. Rather, I am interested in the act of confession, which is itself something worthy.

Memories are family stories. We all have our collection, repeated with humor or embarrassment. Some of them have meaning only to the members of the family, and some of them only to ourselves. For example, there was one person in our family who once laughed with a mouthful of cold potato salad. This was the height of gross behavior, and my mother mentioned it at different times so we could laugh at this person's expense. This person was so unaware, so gauche, that he laughed with his mouth full of potato salad. No matter how many times my mother told this story, we always laughed.

Other memories are fragments, impressions—the squirrels and blue jays playing in the tall, twin oaks in our front yard in Great Kills. The gentle slope of Samson Avenue where in the winter we would belly flop onto our sleds and speed down the hill, making a right turn in front of our house and continue down the slope of Katan Avenue. These are important when you look at them in terms of impressions, emotions, senses. They are not literary mementos, but real-life experiences.

If I dig into my family history, I recognize that my parents gave me the impression that I did not exist on my own unless they confirmed my good standing. If they rejected me, I simply did not exist. At the same time, those memories are there—are they only surface impressions?—of that ignorant, innocent family group that comprised the Guarinos. It's not black and white. In forgetfulness, I remain bitter; when I remember the details, I have to forgive them. After all, it was just life.

We love our lives, our bodies, our memories, because we live inside these bodies. If we were dead, we wouldn't remember belly flopping down Samson Avenue or watching television with our parents. A dead body doesn't remember. It is the soul misidentified with matter that experiences the joy of shouting on a cold day or the pain of rejection. Therefore, our memories are sensual, not the memories of our participation in *kṛṣṇa-līlā*, but they are the signposts that assure us that the soul exists.

Kṛṣṇa teaches that we are attached to the body because the soul is present and because the Supersoul is within. We are ultimately attached to our connection with the Supreme Soul. Therefore, any expression of attachment is an at first dumb and then groping movement toward love of God.

Most people don't get beyond the dumb stage. If by guru's grace we do get beyond that stage, if our past becomes enlightened, then we will understand that we liked to play in the snow not because of the sensual pleasure, but because of the self. We liked to feel the warmth of family pleasure, to laugh at family jokes, and to be a part of life not because of life itself, but because of the self. The self is satisfied by the Supreme Lord's blessing. All these memories, if understood beyond, culminate in our awakening of association with Kṛṣṇa and His *pariṣads* and returning to Him in His abode.

# I Was Drowning

When I asked some friends to help me in this project by requesting me to speak about different memories, I received this from Dāruka: "Looking back on your life before you were a 'devotee,' do you feel that in retrospect, many of your thoughts and tendencies were those of a devotee, even if not fully developed?"

No, I don't. I was associated with the artists who don't believe in God. If I was looking into Eastern thought at all, it wasn't because I was going to become a devotee of Kṛṣṇa; I was an eclectic, and as an eclectic, I would have settled for impersonalism. Therefore, I can't say I was almost a devotee and that Śrīla Prabhupāda gave me the finishing touches. No, no, I was drowning.

In the first apartment that I rented after being discharged from the Navy, I took LSD one night alone. I cried for hours—uncontrollable waves of sobbing. But it wasn't focused on anything particular. It was just grief and tears and choking sobs. I think I was feeling deep inside myself in contact with a person—not the person my parents had taught me to be, but a person within me who had hoped to find happiness but who had found only disappointment. Here I was, playing the bohemian artist, finally alone and free of the Navy, free to write in the big ledger I had bought for myself in Italy, and I should have been happy. But here I was, bawling and bawling and not knowing why.

When it was finally over, I went out and met my amoral friends at a Jewish delicatessen as if nothing had happened. It was like continuing to live after life is over. Somehow I kept existing. I didn't tell them that I had been crying. I just kept living after I was actually dead—all morality and hope gone, washed away by the tears.

No, Dāruka, I don't think that you could call me a devotee before I met Prabhupāda. What I was, though, was a candidate to receive his mercy because he had come to save the most fallen. I was not a complacent person nor a gross materialist nor a conformist; I was simply fallen.

After I met the Swami, I returned to Avalon one more time. I knew then that I would not have to smoke marijuana anymore. I was free of it and I ran along the beach to celebrate. Swamijī was with me and I was happy to return to him and to my new life on the Lower East Side chanting Hare Kṛṣṇa, going to hear from him again and again, becoming initiated, becoming what he wanted me to be—happy in Kṛṣṇa consciousness.

# He Is God For Me

Devotees often try to analyze how it is that they came to accept Śrīla Prabhupāda as their spiritual master. Was it an instantaneous realization, or something that occurred gradually? For me it was gradual, although I do remember one time when I was sitting along with the others in his room. I suddenly got a very personal feeling that he is God for me. Not that I thought Prabhupāda was God, the source of all, but I thought that he was so great a representative of God that he could give me God. It felt conclusive, not something needing scriptural support to bolster my faith. I grabbed onto it and held it close.

I also remember a much earlier feeling from one of the first times I was in the storefront. After Prabhupāda had finished his program and we were leaving, I made a little prayer to God to please protect this man, because I felt he was such a precious and rare person in this world. My prayer was not the prayer of an educated Kṛṣṇa conscious person—it was more like the kind of prayer someone makes before really learning anything about devotional service—but it was sincere. I wanted God to protect this saint, this valuable God conscious man. I wanted him not to die or be lost to me, nor me to him.

Gradually, gradually I came closer to him and closer to Kṛṣṇa.

# Memories Of Death

Great-aunt Doty smelled *bad.* I mean, her body gave off a sharp odor. I was less than eight years old when I went to her house and stood on the sunny front porch. It faced Giffords Lane, and it was my first visit to Great Kills, Staten Island. Almost fifty years have passed, but I can still smell the sharp, unpleasant odor of her body. Even then I knew it was the smell of old age and death. She sat in a rocking chair facing the street, her wall clock ticking loudly. Those images made a deep impression on me.

Death was something I knew little about when I was young. My six-year-old cousin was killed in Eltingville, Staten Island—crushed and buried by a bulldozer at a building site. At the funeral, my Uncle Mickey was dazed and grieving. He said, "We are sure he is in heaven." Everyone at the wake said that. I reminded my uncle that my cousin had had an imaginary friend with whom he used to talk.

At that time I was in college, self-centered and selfish, and I admitted to myself that I didn't know if his son was an angel or not. I went along with it anyway because it evoked my sympathies. "Certainly he must have gone to heaven to be an angel," I said to my Uncle Mickey. "He was innocent; he did nothing wrong. He was just a child. God took him back." How else could we understand it?

Every year the Guarino family had a Mass celebrated in Brooklyn in honor of my grandfather. Then we would go to the huge cemetery to find the grave. It was just a small, marble stone marked "Guarino, Frank." I wrote a short story about it. Every year on his birthday the Guarino clan gathered, first at Mass in the big cathedral, then at some low-class Italian restaurant with a jukebox. After the meal, the men would open their wallets to pay the bill and then we would get into cars and drive to the cemetery, to the little marble headstone to pray at the grave. It made life hopeful, and it was always a sunny day.

There were times when I thought I was dying too but later found out that I wasn't. I don't really remember how I felt while I was laying on the floor, blood gushing from my forehead where the glass had cut it, my vision blurred. I wonder if I was worrying about dying at that moment. I honestly don't remember.

Whenever I was in a car that suddenly skidded into an accident, I would think, "Here we go!" and then I would wait. There was always time to wait.

Some who have had a brush with death have undergone profound changes in their lives. Most report that they thought they were near God and that they experienced incredible peace. I have no memories like that.

This is an interesting point to consider. Of all the memories we have, perhaps the most important one is what carries us beyond this life. We can remember what it was like to sit on the beach with our parents in a warm breeze eating sandwiches, but can we remember death? What did we do when it came to end our last life? We don't remember; birth erased it from our conscious memory.

When death comes, what good will it do us to suddenly remember the smell and taste of the Skippy peanut butter we ate at the school cafeteria? What good to remember our first love's perfume and how we swooned in her presence? Such memories would only lead us to a next body where we can touch and smell—and suffer—some more before dying once again.

There's a famous story of a man who falls into a well. Just as he is falling, he manages to grab hold of a small bush near the top of the well. The bush cannot hold his weight, but in the last seconds before the roots pull free and the man is plunged to his death, honey drips from a branch and onto the man's tongue. The honey tastes so good and the man enjoys it so much that he loses his meditation on God.

The Buddhist version of this story is similar, only instead of the man tasting honey, he tastes a strawberry. The Buddhists consider the man's ability to enjoy the strawberry despite his precarious position as a moment of enlightenment. After all, once he dies, he will be extinct. Lucky for him he went out with the taste of strawberry in his mouth and a heart filled with happiness.

The *Vedas* encourage us to think of Kṛṣṇa at the end. I imagine myself asking for forgiveness and begging Him to take me with Him. I'll pray for the desire to free myself from the shackles of material desire, which bind me to the cycle of birth and death.

I know I am spouting the philosophy here and that it probably sounds theoretical. That's because I don't remember ever finding myself on the edge of life sliding over to death. Others have had more experience. For example, I remember my Godbrother Gobhaṭṭa dāsa in Santo Domingo who told me that when he felt the car turning over in his crippling car accident, he called out to Kṛṣṇa but realized how his chanting did not come from the heart.

The general response to death usually deals more with the particulars of the death than with what happens afterward. We are afraid of drowning, or we choose particular ways in which we would hate to die. We fear panic and pain and the pang of loss. What are we afraid of, that we will have nothing left when this "spot life" is over?

# The Strand Theater—
# In And Out Of The Purport

Virginia Woolf wrote in her *Sketches Of the Past* that much of our day is spent in a state of nonbeing. She compared it to "cotton wool." Only occasionally do we come to life. It's difficult to remember anything about those periods of deadened sensitivity. Unless we live with a sense of our physical mortality, memory is futile. We have to be going somewhere to get insight and meaning from our own lives.

"Going somewhere" means moving from mortality to immortality. Those of us seeking immortality have the extra burden of choosing not to indulge in anything that does not carry us toward our goal. If we can, we remember Kṛṣṇa as constantly as possible. If other thoughts intrude, we find a way to find Kṛṣṇa in all things.

How great is God who is behind the movements of clouds and by whose will the entire cosmic manifestation has come about. The atheists cannot see His hand; they have seen so much suffering and cruelty that they have come to hold God responsible. They cannot accept their own responsibility for choosing to rebel against God. Although they advocate nonviolence and love and justice, they only contribute to the anomalies of the age because they want the kingdom of God without God.

Kṛṣṇa describes them in the *Bhagavad-gītā:* the scholars, the politically powerful, the asses, and those whose knowledge is stolen by illusion. All of them are so devoid of proper intelligence that they cannot see what is obvious: that God is in control and that man is the cause of the cruelty we see in this world.

I speak against the *duṣkṛtinas*, although I'm afraid of them. Prabhupāda assures us that Kṛṣṇa will protect and shelter us, but that doesn't mean we don't have to fight. Sometimes taking shelter of Kṛṣṇa means we *do* have to fight. Arjuna had that experience.

This said, I'll admit that I'm repeating doctrine, what I have heard from Prabhupāda. My mind is filled with such phrases and I both adhere to them and speak them to others. I'm filled with Prabhupāda's phrases. People don't realize the extent to which this is true of me. I slip his words in as much as possible. It's my hidden agenda. It is how I chirp as Śukadeva Gosvāmī's follower. It's my way to make it sweeter. My memory is filled with it.

Unfortunately, there's still room for other memories. I remember pop songs and eating popcorn at the Strand movie theater. I remember the 1950s version of soda machines. We would put a quarter in the slot and it would jangle so loud as to disturb the entire theater. Then—also loudly—the machine would squeeze out a little syrup and then fill a cup with carbonated water. The machine never got it quite in the right proportion; it usually erred on the side of too much carbonated water and not enough syrup. I remember that taste and I remember that theater. I also remember the old women —they were called "matrons"—who were hired to keep the kids quiet and calm during matinees (a thankless task). I remember the rips in the seats. I remember the big screen and seeing *The Thing* and an Elvis Presley cowboy film and John Wayne on screen.

I remember all that, but what do I do with it? I have to "correct" those memories. They were living moments; I wasn't dead when I experienced them, and therefore the memories continue to live in me. Now I have to give them meaning; I have to get beyond the sensual impressions of the raw data. It's hard, though, because there's a part of me that wants to stand up and say, "The soda tasted horrible! I know because I was there! I was alive!" When I watched *The Thing*, the theater was alive with fear. The "Thing" was a monster from outer space that some scientists had discovered frozen in a chunk of ice. The movie was full of social commentary, with the love and peace scientist trying to make friends with the "Thing," discussion about good and absolute evil, etc. Few of us actually saw the movie because most of us closed our eyes. After the "Thing" was killed, a voice came on and added to our fear. It told us to watch the skies to see whether any enemies were coming. Purport anyone?

# O Daughters, O Sons

Madhu has a virus. We're waiting for it to pass. I suggested he take a Tylenol, but he's above that. Says it's his tummy and it's simpler to drink boiled water and not to eat. Okay.

Remember being sick? Remember being a nondevotee and being sick with life? *Appreciate* that you are not like that now! These midnight lines may not be appropriate

because of the underlying irony.
We expect a *sannyāsī* priest
to simply beat the drum
on time
*paramparā* heigh-ho and
yet I ain't always so. I have an
underlying ocean tow, a limp,
although I'm grateful
to be hanging in there.

Do you remember? Is your pre-'66 life more prominent, or your present post? Hey, get this: "Are memories of any mistakes you may have made as a spiritual master a positive tool now, in that you remember that you don't want them to happen again?" Do you mean, did I learn anything or are my mistakes only causes of anxiety?

O daughters, O sons, my mistakes are tools given to me by the school of hard knocks. I'm sadder but wiser. I don't accept Big Worship now or quickly take on disciples. I don't accept a big house—yet I have not learned how to be free of anxiety. Yes, as the question implies, I do worrisomely chew over what I have done wrong. One guy threatened to take me to court for sending his wife out on *saṅkīrtana*. I confessed wrongs publicly and some said it wasn't enough. They want me to return their *saṅkīrtana* money. Some say they would prefer to see me behind bars.

Always in anxiety. It reminds me of Joseph K. in *The Trial*—the weird scenes as he tries to ascertain his guilt. The scene is long and drawn out as only Kafka could do, and maddeningly filled with disturbed people. Then again, the whole *world* is full of anxiety.

I found no home in the Catholic Church and thought in ISKCON I'd be happy on a bed of straw, but then I graduated to a soft bed, a scholar with troubles and no mortgage to pay. I wander free although I am no saint. Yes, I have learned from my mistakes.

# Calamities

I don't remember ever being hurt with a knife, but I do remember how something jumped from my father's hand in the basement of our 76th Street apartment in Queens. It hit the back of my hand and blood spurted out. I don't remember more than that, but I still carry the scar on the back of my left hand. I have other scars on my right arm and face from the time the plate glass window fell on me at the Glenville Avenue storefront. At least that accident occurred while I was practicing devotional service.

And I was a brave preacher lad. In the hospital while they were sewing me up, I told the doctors and nurses about Haridāsa Ṭhākura being beaten in twenty-two marketplaces. The hospital staff was impressed with my religious calm.

I was a zealous worker in those days. My Godbrother and my young wife were in the waiting room and I told the nurse to let them know I was okay and that they could return to their duties. Later that day, I was released from the hospital with twenty-six stitches and I went back to the storefront alone.

Good God, I can only hope that when future calamities come, I can survive them in the same cool-headed way, chanting Hare Kṛṣṇa, the Nṛsiṁhadeva prayers, something Kṛṣṇa conscious. And if the police and ambulance don't arrive on time and I have to pass away, let me do it thinking of my Lord.

Montaigne writes, and I think it is true, that when you're dying, it's not as worrying as when you are only anticipating death. We each have to prove the truth of that statement ourselves. At the end, let us breathe a sigh of relief that we lived our lives as best we could, in Kṛṣṇa consciousness.

# My First Visit to 26 Second Avenue

Whenever I try to remember my first visit to 26 Second Avenue, I first seem to recall the factual and distant things. I was alone when I entered, and the first person I talked to was Ray (later Rāya Rāma dāsa). It was the summer of 1966.

I had already weathered disappointments and personal bitterness and catastrophes, and I was living on my own after being discharged from the Navy. Actually, I had been living alone for almost two full years, and I was no longer close to Elliot or my other Lower East Side friends. I was working on East 5th Street, near the storefront, and I would pass by it on my lunch hour. Then one day I saw a sign in the window for classes on *Bhagavad-gītā*. I was interested in Eastern philosophy and religion, and the *Bhagavad-gītā* and *Upaniṣads* were part of my eclectic reading repertoire. In those days I would read anything, but I especially liked books discussing the Buddhist or Indian path of truth. I had even read the *Bhagavad-gītā*, although I didn't understand it.

I was a shy guy trying to look hip, but I went in anyway. Being hip meant I was supposed to act cool and like I knew how to do things. I had my life together, I thought—a job, an apartment—but I was reserved and didn't stick with anyone's scene. I thought any scene was not cool because it meant people getting together and being too warm or expressive and everything starting to look "square" and sentimental. A part of being hip was to not show homey emotions. Hip meant listening to jazz and reading only certain types of books. Behind it all for me was that I was shy, looking for love, looking for God, although I didn't know it.

I entered the storefront and saw a small group, already acquainted, waiting for the Swami to come down. I sat apart until someone turned to me and introduced himself. He had courage to come forward as a person. We might think that he was just acting as the Swami's representative, but he reached across my barriers and gave me a little of his warmth, even at the risk of not looking hip. It did get through to me. My exterior shell was a thin one, and I was more inclined to see what was going to happen than to maintain my image.

Then Swamijī came. If I use "religious" language or honorific terms to describe him, please don't mind. It was a sacred time for me. I had just met my beloved spiritual master. Someone could say, "Wait a minute, you're jumping the gun. You didn't consider him 'beloved' the first time you met him. Why not give us what you felt?" It doesn't matter what I felt. I am just glad that I can now feel the emotions of gratitude and security that I went to 26 Second Avenue and met my beloved spiritual master.

And the fact that this memory is true makes me feel elated. It's more important than remembering the weathered wood on the platform of the Bay Terrace SIRT stop. What good will *that* image do me at the time of death? Yes, I remember the smell of country air and the innocence and goodness of those days, but those memories will not save me at death the way a memory of having met Prabhupāda will.

Meeting the guru is a once-in-a-lifetime event. Who can estimate what it means to take up discipleship and to honor it throughout a life. I'm not a disciple of Staten Island or the memories I have of those days. I am not even a disciple of life per se. I am a disciple of Prabhupāda, and I am trying to serve and understand the Supreme Lord. I am also responsible now, as a father is responsible, to teach Kṛṣṇa consciousness and to exemplify the practices. There is so much weight on me, but it has good fruit, all planted and nourished by that first meeting. The drama of that meeting continues as I remain attentive to carrying out its implications.

So much depends on Prabhupāda being true and bona fide. He's proven himself, but so much depends on it. Do you know that poem by William Carlos Williams?

So much depends
upon

a red wheel
barrow

glazed with rain
water

beside the white
chickens.

What does he mean, "so much depends"? That's what he felt, that this is life. I say the same thing: so much depends on Prabhupāda, on his bringing Kṛṣṇa consciousness to us in the West, to his being a bona fide representative of the *paramparā*, to our following him without deviation. So much depended on that first meeting. It was sacred.

The other details I've told: how he reminded me of the Buddha, how he wasn't wearing a shirt and his skin was golden brown, how it was a warm summer day, how he didn't sit on an elevated seat but on the same straw mats on which we all sat, how he handed out *karatālas* and asked us to sing the Hare Kṛṣṇa mantra. He led the singing for half an hour and I "dug" it.

I couldn't understand much of what he said, his accent was so foreign to me then. After the lecture, I exchanged a few more words with Ray and went back to my Suffolk Street apartment. I became a regular at the storefront after that first night.

I was young and fearful, but my going there to meet Prabhupāda was an act of bravery. I was doing my own thing and thank God I was because it meant rebelling against my parents' values, against the U.S. government's whole establishment. It also meant I was smoking pot. But it was that same free spirit that allowed me to drop into a Swami's storefront and chant the mantra. It didn't feel like an established religious activity, and it made me high.

It was auspicious. My bad habits easily disappeared. Although I had tried at other times to give them up, I was always drawn back to them by the lack of comfort I found in my intense life. Giving up illicit sex and intoxication was one of the initial miracles I experienced. I became righteous and went forward sober and clean as one of Swamijī's sons, a serious one. I felt strong from following him and nothing else had ever made me feel that way.

# Mentors

I can't remember anyone before I met the Swami who influenced me to take up spiritual life. Of course, if we think of "spiritual" in a broader sense than we usually define it, there were people who helped me climb out of middle-class mediocrity to something better. None of them, however, would have been pleased to hear that I had become a devotee of Kṛṣṇa. That seems significant to me. How can they be wise mentors if they would oppose my spiritual vocation? Most of those people never contacted me again after I joined the Swami. That is also significant. They were atheists and agnostics; intellectuals, not spiritualists.

But it's not that I wasn't influenced at all. Dr. Alexander at Brooklyn College gave me the confidence to become a writer and helped me to both to grow intellectually and to passionately study the great writers. She opened me to the world of Western thinkers and poets. She was an atheist, a Marxist, a Freudian. She thought faith in God was naive, but she influenced me more than any of my other professors.

I was also influenced by some of my friends—Steve Kowit and Murray Mednick in particular—and by anyone who encouraged me to live the life of artist, writer, and Lower East Side mystic. They usually weren't theists either, but eclectics. We didn't read the spiritual classics. Rather, we revered Céline, Genet, and Kafka.

The Navy influenced me too. I was grateful to be working in the Public Information Office, spared from the more abominable work down in the boiler room or in the gun department. I was lucky, but I can't really say that the experience enriched my life. At the same time, the fact that I was able to endure something horrible made me strong. The Navy also taught me to wait. I didn't really know what I was waiting for, but I learned the skill of waiting.

Therefore, it is not an exaggeration to say that I never met wisdom until I met my spiritual master. Whatever helped me to surrender to him, whether negative or positive, I see in retrospect as a good influence and therefore I often feel grateful to everything that happened to me before I met Prabhupāda. Because my parents had trained me in working man's ethics, I was able to apply the ethic and work for Prabhupāda. My eclectic friends helped me to open up to Eastern thinking. My mother raised me to be a practicing Catholic, and although I was not practicing at the time I met Prabhupāda, I had discipline from years of surrender. All these things worked in my favor. Still, despite all that, Prabhupāda gave me the encouragement and love that only a pure devotee can give.

# Looking Into The Dark

"I like to remember the nights when I was living at home, lying in bed and wondering whether or not Kṛṣṇa was really God and praying to Him to reveal Himself to me. I gained most of my conviction while lying there looking into the dark. Have you had similar experiences?"

I like the image of Mādhava dāsa, then uninitiated, looking into the dark. I know the kind of clarity you can feel at times like that and how you do settle major issues when you find that clarity. Sometimes I find such clarity when I am walking. A good idea, a "light bulb" pops. Somebody once told me that our best ideas come in the "three Bs": the bathroom, the bed, and on the bus. In other words, we don't all become enlightened in official places of meditation. Memories and ideas pop into our heads at all sorts of times. If we think they are important, we should remain alert to them, even when they come uninvited or at odd times.

Memory shouldn't be used just to serve some affair that's now concluded. It should give our lives a cutting edge. For example, we should remember the things we meant to do but didn't. We should remember the emotions we felt at different times and resolve them. To open ourselves to such memories is to be open to life.

Of course, there's a limit to how many memories we can open ourselves up to. It would be too much—too much pain, too much volume, and perhaps too much of a diversion from single-minded Kṛṣṇa consciousness—to remember everything with equal concentration. Those whose minds are many-branched cannot pay close attention to their spiritual aims. Therefore, we use memory to serve the goal of life, and we ask ourselves, "What do I want to do in Kṛṣṇa consciousness?" and, "What am I forgetting to do that I said I would do?"

For example, just yesterday I resolved to increase my reading of Prabhupāda's books to two hours a day. I haven't been able to read that much in a long time. It is a decision that I cannot act on immediately, but I must not forget that I made it. And every day I have to remember to chant my sixteen rounds and three *gāyatrīs*. Is this external? It may appear so, but it requires something deeper. It means I must always remember that I am about to die.

It takes time and attention to remember what our lives are about. Wordsworth defined poetry as "Emotion recollected in tranquility." That seems to be what Mādhava is referring to when he speaks of looking into the dark and praying to Kṛṣṇa to reveal Himself. We're not alone, but sometimes we don't wonder about it until we're alone in the dark. We're often too busy to see what is most important.

Irish Origo states it well in her essay, *Images and Shadows:*

> Just as, in travel, one may miss seeing the sunset because one cannot find the ticket-office or is afraid of missing the train, so in even the closest human relationships a vast amount of time and affection is drained away in minor misunderstandings, missed opportunities, and failures in consideration or understanding. It is only in memory that the true essence remains.

I like her point. We might argue that there *is* no essence and that life means distraction, but that's not true. There is an abiding love, an abiding reality, a deeper meaning to every experience that we can get at if we can just avoid being sucked back into the trivial. If we can find that space, as in Mādhava's night, then we can find the essence again.

I try to hack my way through trivia when I free-write. I just can't wait to descend into a single moment of clarity and Kṛṣṇa conscious remembrance. Mādhava asked whether I have had such experiences, and I have. I still do. I do reach out and try to listen for Kṛṣṇa to reveal Himself in some way, and I do it while "looking into the dark."

# Remembering The Teachings About Transmigration In The Kṛṣṇa Book: Chapters One And Two

I especially remember reading the first chapter of *Kṛṣṇa* book for the first time—the wonderful arguments Vasudeva offers to Kaṁsa to protect Devakī. He says, "Don't be afraid of death." The soul transmigrates from one body to another just as a caterpillar goes from one place to another on a plant. The soul is as steady as the moon in the sky. When the moon is reflected in a reservoir of water, it might appear shimmering or broken, but it is whole in its place in the sky. I was thrilled to read it. Why, then, has it now become tedious? Why can't we hear it with the same enthusiasm we felt when we heard it for the first time? Is it too much philosophy? Although there are higher and higher topics discussed in *Kṛṣṇa* book, even to the summit of *mādhurya-rasa*, that doesn't make Vasudeva's arguments relative or less important.

Śrīla Prabhupāda attended his last Māyāpur festival in 1977. He kindly called me into his room once or twice. I had been his secretary in Bhubaneswar just before he arrived in Māyāpur, and although it was now someone else's turn, I felt connected to him in an intimate way. Not only had I been his servant recently, but I had just been appointed editor-in-chief of *Back to Godhead* magazine. Prabhupāda called me in and played me his dictation of the Tenth Canto's discussion on transmigration. He left me with the impression that because we don't understand that we will take another body in the next life, we don't know how to live this life.

Similarly, Chapter Two discusses material nature, the body, and so on, and it is done in the sweet setting of Devakī sitting pregnant on the floor of Kaṁsa's prison while demigods appear to solace her. Sadāpūta Prabhu has explained to us that such events take place in higher dimensions and that the ISKCON paintings are simplifications of the truth. Of course, the highest dimension is love of Kṛṣṇa, and that cannot be depicted to its full extent.

I remember and cherish that simple dedication to the *Kṛṣṇa* book as Prabhupāda presented it and especially the keen desire we felt in the days when the *Kṛṣṇa* book was first published to understand the philosophy and to preach it both among ourselves and to the nondevotees. It wasn't dry or tedious. We loved each example. We were like children reciting just so we could memorize it and grasp it for ourselves. Let me read *Kṛṣṇa* book and remember the past to benefit my present. Reading *Kṛṣṇa* book with enthusiasm is called *śravaṇaṁ kīrtanaṁ viṣṇoḥ smaraṇam*.

# The End

Shall I explain once more how I tried to contact my mother and how she rejected me? In all fairness to my parents, I have to admit that in a sense, I also rejected them. I didn't even attempt to contact them for years. I guess I expected them to contact me. Probably they felt it was my duty to keep in touch with them. Years went by with neither of us making a move toward the other.

In 1977 in Los Angeles I met a woman named Rose Forkash. She was the mother of a devotee, and she served as an intermediary between the devotees and their estranged parents. Anyone who was interested in contacting their parents could give her information about their parents and she would call them and try to bring about a reconciliation. Many devotees accepted her help, and I too went to her one day and gave her the details on my parents. I also confessed that I had just been too afraid to call them over the past ten years.

The last time I saw my mother was in 1967. She and my mother-in-law visited my wife and me in Boston. I had thought the visit went well—my mother bought a suit for me and a drafting table for my wife, and we showed both mothers around the storefront, which was filled with Jadurāṇī's paintings. Later, we took them to our apartment, which, although sparsely furnished, was warm and sunny. But I was wrong. I heard later through my mother-in-law that my mother had been horrified by her visit. I was hurt by her reaction and didn't try to contact her again.

It wasn't only hurt, however. I was more than fully occupied by all my temple duties. Prabhupāda said nothing to indicate that I should cultivate a relationship with my parents. Rather, he wrote me and said that my relationship with my material father was ephemeral and that my relationship with him, my spiritual father, was real.

As the years went by, it seemed to get harder to even think of calling them. When the anti-cult movement gained momentum in the late 1970s, I could only imagine how it affected my parents' vision of what I was doing, and that made it even harder. Up until that point, they had no one with which to share their chagrin that their son had joined a weird Indian religion. Now it was being broadcast on television and in the newspapers: the Hare Kṛṣṇa movement was a dangerous cult, as insidious as the Moonies and the Children of God. I'm sure they were mortified. I wonder what they told people if anyone asked what I was doing. What *could* they say? They probably acted as if I had died.

I also felt that I had broken the family honor and therefore I was no longer eligible to be their son. One devotee, a mother of three, wrote me recently: "As a mother, it is incomprehensible to me how it would be possible to reject one's child, no matter how strongly one disagreed with what they were doing." She cannot think in terms of having a code of honor; if a child were to break that code, the only way he could compensate for it would be to give up his rebellion and to again accept his parents' definition of life. This certainly would have been true in my case. For me to reestablish harmony with my parents, I would have had to either deny or compromise my relationship with Prabhupāda.

There was one other alternative, but I wasn't prepared to accept it. That is, I could have gone to them and begged for their affection. I could have taken their crap directed at me and the Kṛṣṇa consciousness movement—kept taking it—until they finally gave up, if they ever did. I know I would have had to listen to Prabhupāda being blasphemed because that's the kind of people my parents were. They would slur any race or religion or anything outside the bounds of what they considered normalcy. How much of it could I have borne? They never actually said anything blasphemous to me, but I'm almost sure it would have come to that.

The signs were on the wall from the beginning. I phoned my father one evening after the Sunday feast. I felt really happy and I wanted to share my happiness with him. He was incredulous. "A feast? What did you have, three peas and a string bean?" Always sarcastic, and always putting me down. My sister was just the same, but without the profanity that my father usually used, expert needler that she was.

With my mother and sister, the big affront was that I had given up Catholicism for Kṛṣṇa consciousness. I had tried to preach to my sister on the telephone about how faithless everyone was in this age, and I added, "Even the Catholics don't follow the Pope." Although she didn't tell me at the time, I later found out that my statement had offended her. She told my mother, "Who is *he* to say that Catholics don't follow the Pope? *He* doesn't follow the Pope!" She saw it as my hypocrisy, me, the lapsed Catholic. Of course, I was speaking in a broader sense and trying to explain that no one in Kali-yuga follows their religious teachers. My point was that

I had now found a bona fide religious teacher. I expected them—and this was incredibly naive of me—to accept Kṛṣṇa consciousness as if it were a version of Catholicism, a form of love of God. I thought they would appreciate that I *was* a lapsed Catholic. I had committed sinful activities. Now I had given that up to pursue spiritual life. *In essence* I was following Jesus and the Pope. They couldn't swallow it. They preferred me to follow the Pope externally, hypocritically, and at least pretend to be a Catholic rather than join some crazy Indian religion.

My sister thought Indians were worthless people. She remarked on this, coincidentally, the same summer that I met Prabhupāda. I don't really know why she had a prejudice against Hindus, but she listed off a variety of races and what they had going for them, and then she said that Hindus didn't seem to have anything going for them either materially or spiritually. For me to join a religion followed only by the world's poor seemed insulting to her. After all, the white Americans had worked so hard to make a decent place for themselves. All glories to the Irish and Italian-Americans and their climb to the top!

I never knew for sure who was the most stubborn about the freeze between me and my parents. Were they willing to lose their only son just because he joined the Hare Kṛṣṇa movement, or did they decide to reciprocate with what appeared to be my own desire to leave them behind? I expected my father to be tough about my choice, but maybe he wasn't. One of the very few times I talked to him on the phone after joining Prabhupāda, he said, "I'm gonna keep my anchor in with you." He said he wouldn't abandon me, but wanted to keep connected. It touched me at the time.

For these reasons, I can't quite put the whole thing together. Maybe my mother in her apparently quiet and feminine way was the tougher of the two. Because of her religious dogma she thought that I should be cut off and allowed to go to hell. My father, not being so religious, may not have been so hardhearted about it.

Anyway, I suppose it was too much, but I expected them to look me up by looking up the Hare Kṛṣṇa movement. After all, they knew I was in Boston. But I realize that the same thing could be said of me: I knew where they were.

When people hear me describe my alienation from my parents, they assume that we must not have been close even before I joined Prabhupāda. That's not true. I was malleable in my parents' hands. I did whatever they expected of me. While some kids leave home while they're still teenagers, I was part of a more backward generation where kids grew up much slower. We didn't dare to rebel while we lived at home. It wasn't until I was twenty-two and had gone into the Navy that I left home—as their son. The Navy provided me a perfect bridge to leave my parents and to strike out on my own. The Navy also made me resent my father's interference in my life, which caused me so much suffering, and it gave me status as an adult. As soon as I got out of the Navy, I planned to move straight to the Lower East Side and to live out my dream to become a bohemian artist. I didn't even plan to visit my parents first, although I did stay in touch with them.

Anyway, the Hare Kṛṣṇa movement provided a final break, and I guess by then, I was no longer feeling the need to have their endorsement for whatever I chose to do with my life. Besides that, Swamijī invited me to identify myself fully as his son and to spend twenty-four hours a day planning how to spread Kṛṣṇa consciousness.

In 1977 when I met Rose Forkash, I hoped she would bear the brunt of my parents' feelings and that afterwards, they and I could talk. Within twenty-four hours, however, I had a change of heart. I felt I didn't want to open myself to my parents. I was afraid of it. I thought that they might drag me backward into some kind of emotional dependency. I was enjoying my status as a *sannyāsī*, a leader in the Kṛṣṇa consciousness movement, the editor-in-chief of BTG. I was free to dedicate all my emotional energy to Kṛṣṇa. My parents represented something completely opposed to all that. I would have to start by pleading with them to understand my life-style. I admire those devotees who go through all that and who tolerate it because they realize that their parents are spirit souls who need Kṛṣṇa's mercy as much as anyone. I just didn't feel strong enough to do it. I wanted to maintain my emotional freedom. Therefore, I went back to Rose Forkash, took back my information, and said I just didn't think I was up to it.

Again years went by, and of course I didn't forget my parents. I even still dream of them. One of my most frequent dreams is that I'm returning to our home on Staten Island—I'm usually somewhere on the outskirts of New York City trying to catch a train to bring me to the Staten Island ferry. I usually don't make it; I get lost. When I described this recurring dream to a devotee friend, he suggested that maybe I should try to contact my parents. He said that as far as he could see, the relationship was closed, but since I had a haunting sense about something unfinished, it might be worthwhile seeing what it was.

I took it as a challenge. I devised a plan to phone my mother. I didn't know for sure if they were still living or where, but with a little research, I found out that they had moved to what was once their second home in Avalon, New Jersey. I hooked a tape recorder to the telephone so I could record the conversation. My mother answered.

"Is this Catherine Guarino?"

"Yes."

"This is your son," and with an infinitesimal pause I added, "Stevie."

"Yeah." Is was anticlimatic, unloving, a "yeah" full of reservation. I immediately saw it from her side. I know that she was always afraid of people taking advantage of her. She and my father were cynical about the world. They thought the world was full of cheaters ready to take their money. Even though she had to admit that this was her son's voice, she didn't suddenly burst out with an affectionate welcome. I couldn't expect that. After her noncommittal, tough, old woman "Yeah," I said haltingly that I had wanted to get in touch with them because it has been so many years since we'd spoken.

My mother then asked, "Where have you been?" and her voice had a little more human emotion in it.

I told her that I had been traveling all over the world. Then I decided to be blunt. I didn't want her to doubt what I had been doing. "I've been traveling as part of the Hare Kṛṣṇa movement."

That, of course, was the fatal remark. She said, "As long as you are with them, we don't want anything to do with you."

And that's the line that no one can believe. How could she say such a thing? I, too, cannot imagine how she could say it. It's the stand they took throughout the decades: "*As long as you are with them, we don't want anything to do with you.*"

I pleaded a little: "But there are so many sons or daughters who grow up and they turn out to be different than their parents think, but that's not a reason to cut them off." She weakened when I said that. Another, "Yeah . . . " but not with the same toughness.

Then it was up to me. I could have bullied her, I could have begged for her love, but I didn't want to take unfair emotional advantage of her. I also wanted her to accept me as I was.

I know my mother was afraid that I was calling her to sponge off her. They had always thought like that. It was even partly justified because when I was a hippie I went to see them mainly to get money. I wasn't doing that now, but I'm sure it was in the back of her mind. Why else would I be calling after twenty years of silence? Maybe I was down and out and needed a few bucks. Or maybe I thought that they were about to die and I was due an inheritance.

Then I said, "I heard that you were asking for me a few years ago." That was true. When I was traveling quickly back and forth between temples during the zonal *ācārya* days, a message was passed to me secondhand from a devotee at the Philadelphia temple saying that my mother was trying to reach me. When I tried to track down the source of the message, I couldn't find out for sure who had said it or where the information had come from.

I didn't follow up on it. I believe that I wrote a letter to my mother saying that I heard she was trying to get in touch with me, but I never sent it. I somehow thought that I was famous enough in the Hare Kṛṣṇa movement that if they actually called the Philadelphia temple, they could track me down. As soon as I got a definite message, I would call them back. I wasn't really sure about that message, but I mentioned it.

Her reply was surprising: "I *never* did such a thing!" She seemed to be insulted, as if I had accused her of something horrible. It was almost as if she had been steeling herself against any such act. If anyone had suggested to her that she ought to get in touch with me, she was ready to argue her position: "How *dare* you suggest such a thing?"

How can I account for such a harsh and curt rejection? To be honest, I felt immediate relief as she spoke. There wasn't much more to say. In fact, my mother started to reach for a closing line, "All right?" She meant, and may have repeated, "We don't want to have anything to do with you, understand? All right?"

That was it. The conversation lasted two minutes. I think I also told her that I was in Ireland and that sometimes I spoke with different priests.

To that she replied, "I know."

That was strange and unaccountable. Of course my mother's mother is from Ireland, so she may have been interested in my being there. When I said I was in Ireland, she said, "Oh," as if putting one and one together on something that she had already thought. (There are reasons why she might suspect that I was connected to ISKCON in Ireland, but I won't go into that now.)

Anyway the phone call was almost over and I ended by saying, "God bless you." I think she said, "You too," or, "Thank you," and that was it.

Oh yes, I also asked her if she could tell me how the others in the family were doing and she said no.

I was stunned, but I saw it as a blessing from Prabhupāda and Kṛṣṇa. As soon as the phone call was over, I felt a rush as my identity as a devotee returned. After all, I was a Hare Kṛṣṇa, a disciple of Prabhupāda, and not the son of Catherine Guarino. She confirmed it, and after hammering in the last nails, sealed the coffin on the relationship.

Most devotees assure me that this is all Kṛṣṇa's arrangement to help me avoid entanglement in family life. Maybe Kṛṣṇa spared me because He saw how malleable I was and He wanted me to aspire toward higher duties. I hope only that I haven't failed Kṛṣṇa in the opportunity and privilege He has given me to be free of such bondage.

# My Intention To Remember

Memories rise up in the consciousness like dreams—evanescent. They come and go. Unlike our dreams, they are things that actually took place. They are objective, even if our perception of them is subjective.

Examining our memories validates our experience. Since I have lived as a practicing devotee for thirty years, there is much I could examine. I once heard a Godbrother say that our direct memories of Prabhupāda are like precious jewels. He said he had neglected his own jewels but now he wanted to share them.

My question is, why assign value only to the times when we were in Prabhupāda's direct association? Is it more valuable to remember the time we sat in a class with two hundred other devotees while Prabhupāda lectured and then watched him descend from the *vyāsāsana* and drive off in a waiting car? Or, if we were lucky enough to get closer, the time we handed him his cane and he nodded in our direction or asked us our name? Aren't all these years of serving his *vāṇī* in separation equally valuable? Isn't our service to the spiritual master's order working under the same principle as fully ripened *vipralambha*? Yes, but now it is unripe. The *gopīs' vipralambha* has fully blossomed and is bearing the fruit of love of God. Still, in both cases there is union and separation, and in both cases there is happiness. Now, our memories are the ways in which we experience union. We must remember or die.

I remember flashes—a *kīrtana* in the Boston temple in 1976. They had two strange horns, long and twisted, shaped like those we see in some paintings depicting Lord Caitanya's *kīrtanas*. Our library party was visiting Boston for the weekend and I remember Suhotra dāsa Brahmacārī playing one of them during the *kīrtana*.

Our party was welcome in almost every temple we visited because we were touring America selling Prabhupāda's books at the universities and the devotees appreciated our service. We went to Denver and danced up and down the temple room during *ārati*. The temple president said we had brought life to his temple by our visit.

At each university we would approach the main specialist on "Hinduism." If he gave us a recommendation for a standing order, the library would take the books. One day we were all walking onto a campus and one devotee decided he would go and see the prominent professor. I said no, Ghanaśyāma dāsa would do it. That was my role—I was the director.

Once in the Midwest when I was traveling with Hṛdayānanda Mahārāja, we suddenly decided that we should immediately drive to Los Angeles to see Prabhupāda. That was a time when service in separation seemed too slow and we grabbed for Prabhupāda's association almost impetuously. We were so near—only a few thousands miles away—and we knew it was a once-in-a-lifetime chance. When we came into Prabhupāda's presence, Hṛdayānanda Mahārāja admitted to Prabhupāda that the college students were not so receptive. "It is disappointing," Prabhupāda said, commiserating and perhaps hinting that we were not enthusiastic enough in our service, or that perhaps we should find a better way to do it.

I also remember the letter he wrote outlining the ideal behavior of a traveling preacher going to colleges. He described principles of cleanliness and neat appearance and told us to write down our realizations every day to make our preaching sharper.

Do I remember what I was then? Do I remember the happiness I felt when he reassured me with his words and his glances, when he called my name and told me what to do? It seemed so necessary then.

In Chicago, Jagadīśa asked if he could take *sannyāsa*. Prabhupāda said, "Not yet."

Virginia Woolf wrote that when she wrote her memoirs, the past became more real than the present. She got up from her desk and went out to where the gardener and the handyman were working, but the past remained luminous. I have the same experience.

# Irish Devotees

I asked some of the devotees who were asking me questions about my own memories to give me some of their own. As I read their memories, I realized that I have come to know them only in a gradual way. I guess this is how any teacher faced with a large class comes to know his students. The students have only one teacher to get to know, but the teacher has to get to know a hundred students. Over time the students begin to distinguish themselves to him by their various personal traits, and in some cases, their personalities become indelible parts of his life. That is how relationships are formed.

Dīna-dayārdra remembers a time when she was still Bhaktin Deirdre. She had been in the temple for only a month when she saw me for the first time. After a lecture, I asked the ladies for questions. A few of the "older mothers" asked questions. "And then you looked at me and said, 'Do you have any questions, Bhaktin Deirdre?' I couldn't believe it. I was nobody in the temple. People hardly knew I existed, and you, the spiritual master, knew my name. I blushed from head to toe and mumbled some question. I think I grew about ten feet with joy."

I remember this incident too. I think I was proud that I could pronounce her name (although someone had already cued me). Maybe it was part of my sentiment (some would say sentimentality) about the Irish. I don't think there's a more Irish name than Deirdre, and she looked so Irish with her red hair and freckles. Her two children look as Irish as she does.

I'm glad I am no longer relating to these Vaiṣṇava men and women as vague presences who do some service that I recognize from a distance but whom I know little about. I am particularly gratified that they accept me as I am too and that I am able to come here and write peacefully in their midst.

# We Are Family

"Before I moved into the temple, it was my service to make garlands for Rādhā-Mādhava. I used to go to the temple every day, but my mother wouldn't let me move in because she thought I was too young. A devotee gave me a lift to the island one Sunday because there was going to be an initiation ceremony. When I arrived on the island, Mother Madrī asked me to make a garland for you. I was delighted to do it and made a garland of daffodils. My husband was initiated that day and I still have a picture of him placing his banana in the fire with you sitting on the left wearing my garland. Of course, I didn't know that I would be marrying this man, but this picture seemed to connect us together."

There it is. Paste it into your album of memories. It's innocuous. No one will be hurt by it. Later it may become developed and look richer—that saved photo. The same devotee remembers incidents where I interacted with her children. Once I lifted her son up in my arms. Once I laughed as one of her children ran after the pet dog and pulled its tail. Once I held her boy's hand as we walked around the Govardhana Hill they had constructed in the temple room. We are family.

My request for memories drew this one from a young boy in the *gurukula:* "Once I brought my toy gorilla to class and you said, 'Oh, he looks like Dvivida gorilla!' Then you picked him up and started boxing him. I was going to ask you this question in the last class. You said it was not good to follow *avadhūtas*, but Lord Nityānanda was an *avadhūta*. Wasn't Lord Nityānanda a great devotee?" He was sharp to have caught that.

# Don't Be Ashamed Of Love

Why not tell of Hare Kṛṣṇa dāsī's memory of the time she gave me a sagging sweater? Their memories tell of their love and service, but can I face it? Why not?

I think of one who hates me and who thinks I'm misleading persons by taking the position of spiritual master. I wonder where I'll wind up if these ill-wishers have their way. Will I end my days in ignominy, in some dungeon, punished?

I face my infatuation with rock 'n' roll as a teenager and laugh; I face my parents' ignorance and realize that they also cared in their own way. I face *some* of my mistakes and hope my acknowledgment of them will serve a good purpose. Do I dare write of my disciples' affection for me? It too is a testimony. Certainly their love is nothing to be ashamed of.

"I was knitting my husband a woolen jacket. You were leaving the next day. Uddhava said that since the jacket was nearly finished, why didn't I finish it that night and give it to you? Somehow the neck of the jacket turned out really loose. The rest of the jacket was okay and I even managed to put the zip up the front without too much difficulty, but by the time I had knitted the collar onto the already sagging neck, it was obvious that something had gone wrong. Anyway, there was no time to undo it and have another go, so Uddhava gave it to you in that state. (I don't know if you remember it—it was a rich, brown, thick wool, very plain, with a zip front and a saggy neck and collar.)

"We all went to the Dublin airport to see you off the next day. We had arrived first and were waiting for you to come. Then the car came and you got out—wearing the jacket! The neckline sagged almost to your shoulders and I was mortified to have offered you something which had so obviously failed. Then I felt a wave of gratitude. Even though the jacket was a disaster, you had accepted my offering. I could understand that although the result wasn't great, you had accepted my desire to give this to you, and my heart swelled with affection and gratitude."

# Do You Remember In Ireland When—?

"We remember you, Guru Mahārāja, when you came into the temple that day on Crow Street. You wanted strawberries, but your secretary said they weren't good for you because they used to make you break out in hives. You said it wasn't true. Then we felt foolish and decided not to always listen to your secretary but to hear from you directly."

I remember going to that temple that was on the second floor. That was the year I told them not to use the name "Gurupāda" anymore. No one who wrote me their memories mentioned that visit, but I remember it. They remembered that I was a *sannyāsī* and that when I arrived at the Dublin airport one time, the devotees were delayed and no one was there to meet me. Baladeva took me to the temple in a taxi, but when I arrived, there was only one *mātājī*, who had been left behind.

Another man wrote that he knew he had displeased me because he had broken the regulative principles. He came to see me at the airport anyway and I embraced him. I remember that too.

I remember eating scones with butter and talking with Pṛthu Prabhu. Śeṣa Prabhu was my secretary in those days, and he was very, very quiet. As the three of us shared our meals two or even three times a day, Śeṣa Prabhu remained silent. I was embarrassed then that my secretary seemed to have nothing to say, but now I appreciate his gravity. Why talk?

One of the first times I came to Ireland we went out to a peat bog on a hill. It reminded me of a moon landscape. People had been assigned plots where they could dig peat from the earth to use as a heating fuel. Somewhere nearby was a place people considered the devil's. It was supposed to be haunted. An American *brahmacārī* crossed the line and later said that this indiscretion caused him to fall down into illicit sex.

A book for spiritualists should have a purport to every sentence. I shouldn't leave anything to the reader's imagination, they say. Spell it all out and conclude it with *siddhānta*. Someone objected that I related how Madhumaṅgala said he still felt patriotic emotions for the Irish Republicans who opposed the British hundreds of years ago. The critic said I should have added a purport that this sentiment was in bodily consciousness and I should have corrected Madhu on the spot and warned my readers as to what was what. Then no one could accuse me of writing an ambiguous book.

Well, you know what I think about that.

# A Defense of Memories

Although I said that remembering the past is useful and is a sign of life, I would like to add that we should still be careful in how much we value the various memories. We have committed so many destructive and sinful acts in this lifetime, especially in our youth, that remembering them all has questionable value.

Young people tend to be wasteful. Prabhupāda said that the more sinful and extravagant we were in youth, the more we would suffer in old age. Persons who indulged too much in intoxication when they were young may be seriously hampered in spiritual life. Someone who wasted his energy in illicit sex will have to remember those acts again and again. The brain is affected by our youthful craziness and it is then difficult to be steady in devotional service. We also suffered traumas as we grew up in our families, and they too can possibly affect our attempts at devotional service adversely. We were wrong and we were wronged. Serving Kṛṣṇa is completely transcendental, but we are stuck under the modes along with our particular warped impressions of the past.

Do we remember our own past simply as therapy, then? No. If I'm going to stick to my original premise, then I have to say that we don't have to psychoanalyze ourselves when we remember. My point now is that neither should we remember as unredeemed hedonists.

Rather, we should trust the memory process to bring us closer to Kṛṣṇa.

Is anyone shaking his head, not understanding what I'm saying? I keep speaking about this because I don't completely trust my readers' comprehension. I'm also afraid someone will misuse what I am saying to defame me or the Kṛṣṇa consciousness movement. That sort of thing. Or, because I'm not writing purports to all the memories, it's likely that if I tell a memory not centered on Kṛṣṇa, certain devotees will wave their fingers at me admonishingly and say, "Anything that doesn't explicitly center on Kṛṣṇa is *māyā*. You're leading people into *māyā*."

I don't think they're right, but it will require my trust and yours to get past these obstacles. In other words, I know that the things I say will be available to unsympathetic readers, but I have to say them anyway in order to reach those who will appreciate and make a similar attempt. It's a saintly attempt. Being saintly doesn't always mean treading the well-paved road of recited scriptures; it also means sharing some honest notes about the struggle. The struggle means "where we've been." Without looking at our memories, how can we feel gratitude, repentance, even happiness or sadness? Looking at our memories helps us to live our lives in context instead of as a series of disjointed events that we rubber-stamp "Kṛṣṇa conscious."

With that in mind, here are a few things that came to mind today. I worked for two successive summers as a Parks Department boy on the beach at Great Kills Park. We wore orange pants and a green T-shirt as a uniform, and a green, beaked cap. There were various duties involved with the job, and we were supposed to take turns doing them all. We were to pick up trash with a nail on the end of a pole, and we had to collect tickets at the bath house and drive around on a beach vehicle picking up wood and trash. It was certainly an easygoing job, and it wasn't unusual for us to hide out for hours in the afternoon and not do anything at all. Our bosses didn't seem to mind.

That was the summer that I used to drink Coca-cola and eat hero sandwiches for lunch, and I read great literature. I thought so many things.

From that memory, I suddenly remembered my mother's refrigerator. She used to tell us that she didn't really know how to cook, although there were certain things she made that I definitely liked—lemon meringue pie with whipped cream, chocolate pudding pie with whipped cream. She made other things too, but as Prabhupāda says in his lectures, "We don't want to discuss." I couldn't judge her cooking overall; my father said that when he married her, he had had to teach her how to cook and she never protested that account.

She was a churchgoer, though, a Catholic. She did not read the Bible much. Because of her religious beliefs, she didn't drink much or smoke. While we didn't speak of her more private life, I found out later from my father that she preferred to be celibate than to engage in an intimate relationship with my father. My father actually confessed that to me near the end of my days with them. My mother never showed the slightest interest in any other man, but she was not a nun. She was a Manhattan-raised kid and loved the excitement of city life. I don't think it was only because we needed the money that she took a part-time job as a clerk at the Chase Manhattan Bank. Rather, she was bored sitting in our house in Staten Island, city girl that she was.

When she went to the city, she would dress stylishly—high-heeled shoes and a skirt that revealed her shapely legs. Although she was chaste, she liked to move around in the city and be seen as a woman in the office. She enjoyed that sort of worldly exchange. In other words, she was a *karmī* wife.

I am saying all this only to say that I didn't really know her well. I tend to think that if I begin to uncover the details that I remember, I might find some surprises. I suspect she was a tough person, unloving, but of course, I might think like that because she rejected me on the flimsy grounds that I joined a strange cult. My friends are always shocked by her behavior. When Baladeva heard a recording of the two-minute conversation I had with my mother after twenty years of silence, he said that she sounded hard-hearted. She reminded him of some crusty old aunts of his from New Jersey. Yes, she had a tough heart. She was ready to kick out a son who didn't measure up to presentable standards. She had a rigid idea of what was acceptable, and she abided by the law laid down by her husband. That's how it was and that's how it would have to be. I tend to think she didn't know how to love.

But I don't want to fall into that conception too easily. After all, she has her own side to the story. She could accuse me of trying to sponge money from them or blame me for not being grateful. She was hurt, even mortified, when I broke away from them after the Navy and went to live on my own on the Lower East Side. She had spent her life planning for my middle-class life. I rejected her values and she couldn't accept it. These were the grounds upon which she rejected me. She wanted me to be normal, to get married and have a family, to bring the grandkids by on holidays. She didn't want me to be a hippie, which I became up until I met Prabhupāda, and she certainly didn't want me to join a cult. It was too much.

Middle class values were deeply inscribed in both of my parents' lives. My father was the son of immigrants. It took a lot of work to climb beyond their low-class economics to the top of the middle class. He worked hard for that second house. If my mother was tough, my father was tougher. She shared his vision and clung to him and his tough, American, non-liberal attitude. Neither of them liked people whom they considered beneath them economically or culturally. She didn't like Asians or street beggars, for example. They believed in survival of the fittest and they were proving themselves fit to take care of themselves, pay the bills, fight off the world, and to shape their little family clan around identical values. The Hare Kṛṣṇa movement was just too much for both of them.

Dear Mom, I have many sweet memories of you. I'm made in your image in many ways, and I know I can't escape those traits. They surface from time to time. I won't reject you as you rejected me. You are a Catholic and you aspire for heaven; I am practicing Kṛṣṇa consciousness and aspiring for the spiritual world. Best we don't curse each other but see the common thread in our aspirations and wish each other well. Or perhaps you don't wish me well. Still, despite your curse I bless you, as I did the last time we spoke on the phone: "God bless you." I thought you might understand.

# Madeline

When I used to hear the sadness of the blues, the smoothness, the sweetness of a musical arrangement with drums, bass, alto sax, piano, and trombone, and with that unique Charles Mingus inspiration, I would want to share it with someone close to me—my sister, or someone like her.

When I was young, I would bring Madeline to the Staten Island jazz club where great jazz musicians played on Sunday afternoons, or to a concert in Central Park. She wasn't avid about jazz like I was, but she was willing to share my appreciation. She knew, as I did, that jazz was about something more than making music; it was about art and emotion and life. That's why it never seems enough to enjoy art alone; we want to share our appreciation with others. In fact, the experience of art doesn't seem complete until we have shared it with someone else and our experience has been authenticated.

My sister knew about emotion. Although I often characterize her as cynical and mocking, she was an emotional person. She had a heart murmur; she was good-looking, intelligent, and popular; but she was helpless, almost weak in some ways; and she was feminine.

My father loved and protected her. That was the cause of some of our sibling rivalry. When she was a baby, my father would sing tenderly to her a song with the refrain, "And she's daddy's little girl." I don't remember him singing such songs about his son. Madeline and my father had little things that they shared. For example, they both loved olives. I *hated* olives. Whenever I was offered olives by the members of my Italian-American family, I would always refuse them. Then my father would turn to Madeline and she would eat as many as he would give her.

I remember a photograph of Madeline taken at Forest Hills Park that I always liked. She was sitting on a park bench, her upper lip white with ice cream, and she was wearing a pinafore. She was only about six or seven years old in the photo, and looked darling. I was proud of the fact that my sister was so pretty.

Although she was not particularly protective of me, she protected me in high school by going ahead of me and establishing herself with a good reputation. She was a cheerleader and ran for high school president and did other appropriate things so that by the time I got to high school three years later, I wasn't a nonentity; I was Madeline's little brother. Her boyfriends were seniors at the high school, and that was also to my credit.

Of course, Madeline and I were friends in the way that brothers and sisters are friends. We kept our secrets and had many private talks between us unknown to our parents. She used to confide in me her frustration with our parents. Together as we grew into our teens, we shared the realization that our parents weren't perfect. She was especially critical of our mother, and through this sharing we became more intimate. Her mocking cynicism toward me, however, peppered the intimacy.

I went to college without having achieved the same high grades that she had had in high school. She was admitted to Hunter College, a prestigious university. I couldn't even get into Brooklyn College because my grades were less than average. Instead, I went to Staten Island Community College and decided to major in history. After meeting an exciting English professor, however, I decided to change my major to English, which was also Madeline's major. When I told her, she admitted frankly that she would become envious because I would probably make a better English major than she did. And it was true. I had more of a passion by that time for becoming an intellectual and for loving the poets and writers than she did. My education had gotten off to a slow start, but college revolutionized me. I woke up and began to outdistance my sister in artistic and intellectual pursuits. It's then that her mocking really began, and it was during those years that she began to become more conservative herself.

She knew my weaknesses. "Oh, Stevie," she would say, always putting me down. She was intent on exposing my follies and insincerities, but she did not know the depth of my soul or my sincere love for a life free from the established and conservative values of our parents. Although she too professed her disdain for those values, she wasn't as daring or as idealistic as I was. Of course, I hadn't yet faced the economic reality of needing to pay the bills, but I scorned the *karmī* values and vowed not to sell out to the Establishment. Madeline agreed with my spirit, but it was beyond her to live it. We both saw the words "Sold Out" stamped on the commuters who, like a herd of cattle, rode the trains to the Staten Island ferry every day and then poured into Manhattan by the thousands. We both wanted to avoid that fate somehow or other. In the end, though, she sold out, married a conservative Establishment man, a stock analyst, and saw her dreams of romance go up in smoke.

Their marriage was more one of convenience and economic consideration than of passionate love.

A couple of years before I met Śrīla Prabhupāda, John Coltrane's album, *A Love Supreme*, was released. I called Madeline and tried to convey to her my enthusiasm for what I saw as Coltrane's spirituality. I remember saying, "It's as if the heaviest, most dangerous guy on the block suddenly says he believes in God." My sister scoffed and said, "Why don't you get married?" She seemed genuinely embarrassed whenever I tried to discuss anything of the heart with her. She seemed to become frightened by any attempt at intimacy, and she deflected it with her mocking.

That was the harbinger of what was to come. When I finally met Śrīla Prabhupāda, I didn't dare share it with her; I knew I had found the real thing and I wanted to protect myself from her scathing remarks. After a few weeks of *kīrtanas* and lectures, however, Swamijī told us of his plan to have his disciples cultivate trustees for his young society. The *New York Times*, *East Village Other*, and *National Enquirer* had already published their first articles about Prabhupāda and his band of followers. Śrīla Prabhupāda photocopied these articles and requested his preachers to show these materials to whomever they thought could contribute and then to solicit a donation of about $40 or $50. I couldn't think of anyone to ask. Therefore, I reached out to my sister in a somewhat desperate mood.

Madeline and her husband, Tommy, were living in Westchester, New York at that time. To get there, I had to take the New York Central train. It was a long train ride, but I spent the time reading *Easy Journey to Other Planets* for the first time. By the time I arrived at my sister's home, I was ready to preach. Tommy was still at work, so after some sibling talk, I felt in a naive but genuine way that I should share this knowledge that I had found and that she herself could have. I had a fanatical edge to me, however. For example, I remember telling her that sex pleasure was nothing more than an attempt to squeeze lumps of flesh together. Pleasure was something only of the soul. On and on I went. When her husband came home, I continued unabated. I preached to him with a Christian allusion that Jesus Christ had said it was harder for a rich man to enter the kingdom of heaven than for a camel to pass through the eye of a needle. Tommy immediately got upset by my hammering away and tried to counter me with logic. I pressed on with missionary zeal and then directly asked for money. Tommy flatly refused. Not on financial grounds, he said, but on principle. When I realized that he would not give money, I abruptly decided to leave. They laughed and asked me to calm down. They were looking for the spark of that person they thought they knew. But I was different, and neither did I have the wisdom to behave normally as an act of preaching. Tommy drove me to the train. I tried some last preaching to him on the way. I remember saying, "Don't think of this as some kind of strange sect. It is transcendental loving service."

"Yes, I understand," he said, but he dropped me off at the train rather coldly.

I returned to Prabhupāda as quickly as I could and told him, happily, of my failure to collect the money. Why was I happy? Because despite my fanaticism and bumbling, I had at least remained faithful to Swamijī's lotus feet. Swamijī understood my happiness and gave me *dāl* and *capātīs*. And that was my last contact with my sister.

# Free-write Memory

Kṛṣṇa consciousness is as nice as flowers and tougher than steel. It is filled with people, like Noah's ark, even some you'd rather not be with. Sometimes the *kīrtana* gets too loud for an old guy and he leaves the stuffy room (youngsters don't even seem to be aware of the need for oxygen) and walks outside to circumambulate the building. Other devotees are doing the same. A widow hangs her white cloth on the clothesline.

Lie in bed and think of all the things that might detain you in the material world. Are you thinking, "Look, I'm not going to make Goloka anyway in this lifetime; it's not that only a small margin separates me from perfection. I might as well indulge a little . . . "? But I read somewhere that when you are thinking of quitting, at that moment you might be just steps from the goal. So don't quit striving for perfection, and if you've got a long way to go, then that's all the more reason not to hang back.

Blow your coronet
Ekalavya dāsa,
as Hayagrīva did.
Prabhupāda recalled, "I saw the
coronet lying there and thought of
Hayagrīva dāsa."

A dimple-cheeked *gurukula* girl . . .

Judith Wax wrote an essay called "Raise Your Hand If You're a Spirit Soul." It was published in a national magazine. She and her husband later died in an airplane crash going from Chicago to L.A.

I remember pepper, ground pepper, and all the alternatives to things that aren't good for you—carob instead of chocolate, homemade ice cream instead of store-bought, honey instead of white (skull and crossbones here) sugar. Some call it White Death. One of those who do has a new name now. Is it more *rasika*?

I was asked to spread Jayānanda's ashes in the Yamunā and did so without ceremony. I remember almost drowning—no, it wasn't that bad, just a few seconds of panic—under the metal floating barge in the Yamunā. I should have kept a cool head.

Hundreds of people died in the night club fire, in the airplane crash, in the collapsing building when the U.S. smart bombs made a mistake and landed on top of civilians in Baghdad. Let's change the topic. News articles are secondhand rumors. They might be about events that never really happened.

I remember blues, reds, whites, yellows, phrases like "the flat plains of the Ganges." I wrote a poem on arrival in Māyāpur and mentioned myna birds and those green leaves with yellow striations. I want to tell a certain Māyāpur resident how different I am from him. I am Westernized, but a devotee, and he is attempting to shake off all of his Western identity while living in the *dhāma*. Lord Caitanya has become Gaura to him and he spends every moment with Him. I asked him if he'd read a particular book I had written, but he said he had no money. "If Gaura wants, then I will get it and read it." Is Gaura walking around fulfilling the desires of the residents of Māyāpur? He very well may be. More chance of that than Saint Patrick taking care of us as we drive into Northern Ireland.

I remember buying books in Times Square. I had no guide to tell me what to read, so I bought a book about Private Slovik, the only GI sentenced to death for desertion during World War II. The reporter who wrote it asked why this ordinary coward was chosen to be killed. He didn't do anything *that* bad, but the system demanded his death. I also read *Fads and Fallacies: In the Name of Science*, which debunked Charles Fort, Edgar Cayce, Dianetics, and other "anti-scientific" causes. Why did I choose these books? I was young (in high school) and I wanted to read. Later I read only those books dictated by the intellectuals to be of sufficient depth.

ISKCON days. I opened a letter from Swamijī, read it, and said, "This is wonderful!" Then I shared it in the *prasādam* hall with the other devotees.

*Jeepers creepers, where'd you get those peepers? Gosh, oh, jeepers, where'd you get those eyes?* Pañcadraviḍa Swami once took me aside, and in a confidential undertone, sang that song in imitation of a night club crooner. It was just what I needed to crack me up, to give me a moment of relief from the boredom and torture of the GBC meetings.

We have had plenty of stuff to throw at each other from all sides.

"You did *this*!"

"Yeah, and you did *that*!" That's the history of the Protestants and Catholics in Northern Ireland, the Arabs and Jews in the Middle East, the Indians and Pakistanis, the Serbs and the Croatians, the this-group and the that-group. Someone has to break the chain of "an eye for an eye," Gandhi said, "or the whole world will go blind."

Kṛṣṇa, I'm sorry for what I did. (Am I? I *say* it here, but how deeply do I mean it?) Please forgive me. If I have offended anyone, then let them also forgive me. That would seem to be one of the functions of memory, to recall what we did wrong, to remember those whom we have offended, to walk in their shoes, and to ask forgiveness. "I am fallible. I made a mistake. I suffer from misunderstanding."

Remember history and don't revise it in your favor. Who can say the war never happened? We can say that if we had it to do over, we wouldn't make the same mistake. We have learned something and have become smaller, humbler, freer from malice and judgment because of it.

Is that good enough?

The critics, the victims, the angry, the militant, the pro-activists who just don't like you scream, "No!"

In his memoir, Sigmund Freud writes of how he felt alienated among his contemporaries. He read an essay by a man named Josef Popper-Lynkeus and, because he agreed with Popper's theories and even tried to develop them further, Freud loved him. But Freud was afraid of meeting him because he had been spurned so often.

> A special feeling of sympathy drew me to him, since he too had clearly had painful experience of the bitterness of the life of a Jew and of the hollowness of the ideals of present-day civilization. . . . But I never sought him out. My innovations in psychology had estranged me from my contemporaries, and especially from the older among them: often enough when I approached some man whom I had honoured from a distance, I found myself repelled, as it were, by his

lack of understanding for what had become my whole life to me. . . . So it came about that I put off calling upon him till it was too late and I could now only salute his bust in the gardens in front of our Rathaus.

—"My Contact With Josef Popper-Lynkeus"

Memories. "In his previous birth, Kaṁsa had been a great demon named Kālanemi and had been killed by Viṣṇu. Upon learning this information from Nārada, Kaṁsa became envious of everyone connected with the Yadu dynasty." (*Bhāg.* 10.1.68)

Memories are supposed to mellow us, to make us small and humble and less malicious, less sure in our righteousness, but here the demon suddenly remembers his enemies and tries to kill them—all of them! Nārada gave Kaṁsa past-life recall just to incite him to more quickly fill up the cup of his evildoing so Kṛṣṇa would appear that much sooner.

In the "Additional Notes" to the first chapter of the Tenth Canto, Madhvācārya is quoted on transmigration. He says that when we are awake, whatever we see or hear is impressed upon the mind, which later works in dreams to show us different experiences. We dream in combinations what we experience in wakefulness. When we awake, however, we forget the dreams. "This forgetfulness is called *apasmṛti*. Thus we are changing bodies because we are sometimes dreaming, sometimes awake and sometimes forgetful." Similarly, death creates forgetfulness: "Forgetfulness of our previously created body is called death, and our work in the present body is called life. After death, one cannot remember the activities of one's previous body, whether imaginary or factual." Śrīla Prabhupāda once said that if a sinful person were to remember his sins (and the fact that he has to suffer for them), he would shudder. Therefore, he denies them; he chooses to forget them.

It takes courage to remember. It takes even more courage to remember Kṛṣṇa because remembering Kṛṣṇa means acting out our identity as His servant. Don't sit around with old friends getting intoxicated on sweets and talking ISKCON *prajalpa* or about how you used to be in *māyā*! Be brave enough to remember Kṛṣṇa. Some past memories help and others hinder. Therefore, follow this most important rule: accept what is favorable for devotional service and reject what is unfavorable.

What about this memory: I was walking from the *prasādam* hall in Māyāpur toward what was then the first building. I saw lights over the building arranged to spell the words "Hare Kṛṣṇa." It was during the annual Māyāpur festival and I felt happy to be in Māyāpur and to be part of the Hare Kṛṣṇa movement. It is a simple memory of simple happiness to be a devotee and to be in the holy *dhāma*.

We all have bubbles of optimism about our lives as devotees. We can remember them. I remember experiencing such a bubble once when I was walking around the *parikrama* path in Vṛndāvana. I suddenly realized that I had passed the halfway mark. I was going to make it. All I had to do was to keep going.

# Mom, You're An Ace

When I was a child, my parents bought me a Schwinn bicycle, which, in those days, was considered the best. It came on a UPS truck and was delivered in a large, thin box. It was a beauty, 26 inches tall. I fell in love with it at once, but I was so young and inexperienced that I had no idea how to ride it. Although the bicycle's arrival was a momentous occasion for me, I suddenly felt too afraid to learn how to ride it. My mother, however, insisted that I learn, and now, although I was unwilling, she pushed me to get on it immediately.

I don't remember anyone teaching me to ride. I simply wheeled the bike to the curbside and got on. It was hard because I didn't know how to find my balance, and every time I thought I was going to lose my balance, I would put my foot down on the road and try again. Slowly, shakily, I learned to balance myself and keep my feet on the pedals. Then I began to ride, awkwardly, but down the road.

After that first attempt, I ran back to my mother, who was by then in the kitchen, and said, "Mom, you're an ace for making me ride the bicycle!" I wasn't usually so spontaneous in expressing my feelings with my mother, and usually our exchanges were more dutiful and routine, but this was an *occasion*. My mother had pushed me beyond what I thought were my limits and I had achieved something.

I can just imagine myself telling a story like this to Prabhupāda and his saying something like, "That is natural." Such examples might prove to him things that he felt were ordinary truths and that somehow had a bearing on Kṛṣṇa consciousness. For example, Prabhupāda upheld the standard that parents are wiser than their children. If a child were unwilling to do something that was for his own good, Prabhupāda thought he should be forced. He quoted Cāṇakya Paṇḍita's aphorism that if you are lenient with a child, he will be spoiled. Prabhupāda was aware that in the material world, there were aberrations in the parent-child relationship—there were parents who abused their children or demons like Hiraṇyakaśipu—but he often upheld through analogy the standard relationship of protective parent and dependent, less knowledgeable child.

Of course, he also knew that such ordinary truths were only preliminary to real wisdom. The most important thing a parent has to give a child is Kṛṣṇa consciousness. If the parent cannot bring the child to spiritual life, he or she is not worthy of being called father or mother. If they didn't come to this standard, Prabhupāda considered it all ignorance. My mother wasn't an ace for teaching me to ride a bike after all. The real credit goes to my spiritual master and the Vaiṣṇavas for helping me to sacrifice something of myself, to give up my reluctance and shyness and to reach beyond what I think are my limits to try to serve Kṛṣṇa.

# Perspectives Of Memory

Psychologists and other medical researchers say that the first moments, weeks, and years of one's life are formative. " ' . . . brain cell formation is virtually complete before birth,' and in the months after birth 'the formation of connections among these cells, that allow[s] learning to take place . . . proceeds with astounding rapidity' . . . brain development is much more vulnerable to environmental influence than we had ever expected.' " (*The Anatomy of Memory*)

I wonder how much of this applies to someone who has truly experienced a second birth—who has given up his former life and taken to the spiritual path under the guidance of his spiritual father. It seems an exaggeration to say that the past is completely erased once we meet the guru and start to practice *vaidhi-bhakti* because so many devotees, after a period of initial enthusiasm, succumb to their innate material traits. If we are sincere in our practice of Kṛṣṇa consciousness, however, it is not an exaggeration to say that we have stepped into a different category than those who have never come to the *bhakti* path. We don't want to lean too heavily on psychology in our practice of Kṛṣṇa consciousness, but it seems we have to do whatever is vital and natural to us to make ourselves whole for Prabhupāda. Therefore, we may claim our memories.

I just read in *Sketches of the Past* by Virginia Woolf her description of her very first memory, in a nursery, as a small baby. She says she remembers hearing the sound of the waves on a nearby beach. She says there is no overestimating how important this memory is to her life:

> If life has a base that it stands upon, if it is a bowl that one fills and fills and fills—then my bowl without a doubt stands upon this memory. It is of lying half asleep, half awake, in bed in the nursery at Saint Ives. It is of hearing the waves breaking, one, two, one, two, and sending a splash of water over the beach; and then breaking, one, two, one, two, behind a yellow blind . . . it is of lying and hearing this splash and seeing this light, and feeling, it is almost impossible that I should be here; of feeling the purest ecstasy I can conceive.

Of course, we have to turn to psychology to understand the "enlightenment" of her experience. Her ecstasy was based on her feeling of total security, and she measured all other bliss by this feeling. It's not a God conscious realization, but it shaped her life. A truly enlightening memory would be to remember something that sparks our understanding that we are eternal servants of God. That can come in earliest childhood or at least before death. A New York reporter once pressed Prabhupāda about how old he was when he had his first spiritual realization. Prabhupāda resisted the question and instead began to preach, but the reporter persisted and Prabhupāda finally said, "At four or five years old." This is what has to be imbibed for life to be successful. It's not an intellectual attainment, but it comes from good spiritual education and the association of *sādhus*, and by Kṛṣṇa's grace: "I'm not this body; I'm pure spirit soul."

Do I have such a memory? Is this what I am groping for when I look to my past? How can I expect to find it in the days before I met Prabhupāda? I was twenty-six years old in 1966, which according to psychologists is not only an age where someone is well-formed, but they are actually beginning the downward slide.

Well, then can I look for such a memory since 1966? All I can say is that whatever I am now has been influenced by what I was before. The kind of devotee I am, how submissive I am, how pure of heart I am—it's coming from both my spiritual education and my material conditioning. Spiritual knowledge can, of course, overcome material conditioning, but it might take time. Therefore, some self-awareness of who you were before you came to Prabhupāda is useful. James McConkey, editor of *The Anatomy of Memory*, writes, "We are always what we were; we know ourselves—to the degree that knowledge of the self is possible—through our ever-growing past. . . . memory gives us a double perspective . . . not only does the past inform the present, but the present informs the past. In other words, the understanding of our present selves that memory provides us is capable of returning the gift, enabling us to know our earlier selves in a manner that eluded us then."

In Kṛṣṇa conscious terminology, we might say that although all true knowledge began only when we approached the guru, nevertheless, our ability to assimilate it depends on the awareness of who we were and how we had been formed before we became devotees. Conversely, because of the knowledge we have assimilated since meeting the spiritual master, we can better understand what would otherwise be a confusing and disturbing identity.

# Mādhava Dāsa's Memories

Mādhava sent me a batch of his memories. I liked every one of them. He recalled the time we were together at New Vrindaban in 1983 and when I took part in an oxcart procession with Kīrtanānanda Swami. It was for some big ceremony, and he and I were in the center as gurus. We smashed coconuts on the ground and sprayed the devotees with water. Yes, I remember that. Mādhava said that that night I led the *kīrtana* while four or five hundred devotees all pressed in around me, including many leaders and *sannyāsīs* with whompers and drums. He said, "And you were the center of it all." Actually, I don't remember that exact *kīrtana*, but I remember similar ones. Those days are over. I simply don't have the physical strength and am no longer willing to put myself in the center of a big function like that. Something has died out in me.

Mādhava also recalled the Vyāsa-pūjā ceremony held in my honor in 1982 at the Brooklyn temple and how Hari Śauri Prabhu, then a member of the GBC, led the chanting. It got rowdy. Mādhava, who was still Bhakta Mike at the time, recalled seeing me dragged back and forth up and down the length of the temple room as part of the dancing. He said I didn't seem to like it. Yes, I remember that too. The Vyāsa-pūjā was held in the middle of the Christmas marathon. It was scheduled to be a break for the *saṅkīrtana* devotees, who would then go out enthused to finish the last two or three weeks. I felt

I was being used to inspire them. It was a hopeless time for me then. There was nothing I could do but play the role.

Another memory Mādhava had was of my taking an invalid's retreat in Gurabo, Puerto Rico in 1984–85. I remember that time well, although until he reminded me, I didn't recall his participation in it. He said I was compiling another volume of *Prabhupāda Nectar* at the time. One time he was in the kitchen and heard me reading a humorous story about Prabhupāda and Viśala dāsa. He said Baladeva and I were giggling like children and Mādhava loved it.

Then he remembered a walk we took in Boston in the summer of 1983 in the Boston Gardens. I stopped before each statue and said something. In front of the statue celebrating the invention of anesthesia, I said, "Can this cure death?" Yes, I remember that. During that visit, he brought me a glass of orange juice before *maṅgala-ārati* and I said, "So, Bhakta Mike, do you want to be a devotee?"

"Yes, very much."

He was also there when we tried to take a break in Cape Cod one winter. I wrote *Choṭa's Way* there. I wince to remember how the health department and the police threw us out of there. The police came to Baladeva's cabin one night and interrogated him as to why in hell he was staying in a summer cabin in the middle of winter. A day or so before this incident, a man had come to the cabin thinking the residents were someone he knew. When I opened the door and faced him dressed as a devotee, he was friendly but surprised. He too wondered what we were doing there. He must have complained to the health department and had us thrown out of there.

Mādhava recalled a visit we made together to Jagannātha Purī in 1993. Of course, I also remember that time. He didn't know all that I was going through on that visit, but during that time, I solidified my relationship with Śrīla Prabhupāda and went through other heart changes. Although we say the past is gone, the twinges of memory live on still delivering their little sting. Yes, we are who we were. We are living out the reactions to our past activities.

This is another reason why we need to remember our lives. If we look back, we'll see that we live our lives according to resolutions we made in the past. Change doesn't come easily because not only are we living out the reactions to activities we can see, but we are living out the reactions to things of which we have no conscious memory.

Mādhava acknowledged that some of his memories may not be so meaningful to me. It's true that we can't share with another the intensity of their feelings. We have our own experiences over which to feel emotion. I find it especially difficult to share the depth of another's experience because there are so many persons who take even small incidents with me as important. I want to be big-hearted, but I am only a tiny mortal. Still, I honor their memories.

# Past, Present, And Future

All three aspects of time—past, present, and future—have relevance to a devotee. We exist in the present moment, but the present has been created by the past. Therefore, it is useful to examine the past if only to gain more perspective on the present. At the same time, we don't want to dwell on the past but to spend our time chanting and developing faith in the process of Kṛṣṇa consciousness. The Kṛṣṇa conscious process is greater than the self, and that means it is greater than either our past or our present. We engage in *bhakti* on the cutting edge of now, trying to devote ourselves minute by minute. As each moment flows into the past, we cannot purchase it back for a mountain of gold. And this fact establishes the superiority of the present over the past.

But the past has relevance. By examining the past, we learn to feel regret for time misspent, that time that is irrevocably lost. Such regret impels us forward into the present moment: don't waste it. Knowledge of the past also teaches us the reality of the future. We cannot control the future—it is in Kṛṣṇa's hands—but by looking at the past, we remember that the present shapes the future.

In other words, by living in the present while looking at the past, we see beyond the breaking surf to the swell that's behind it. The more we see the swell, the more impetus we have to live our present to our best advantage. When people live in the present superficially, they live simply to enjoy their senses. They emphasize the now-ness of life as if it is isolated from the past: "To hell with what happened before, and to hell with what comes after. Let us enjoy now!"

A devotee practices *śreyas;* we temper our present activities with knowledge of our reactions from the past and the direction of our future. My dear Lord Kṛṣṇa, I have mistakenly come into this world. Now I want to make amends.

# Diving Out The Window

I remember once reading a passage in something Proust had written. He said a car almost ran him down when he was absentmindedly walking along the street. When he stepped back quickly to avoid the car, he stepped on the paving stones, which were uneven. Suddenly all his experiences in Venice flashed before his mind, not the usual superficial—what I call "canned"—memories, but the impressions that had run deep into his heart and generated some emotion. Our memories are like a kaleidoscope. Just the slightest shake changes the colors and patterns, and everything looks different.

Prabhupāda has explained that the unconscious is like a pool out of which memories and impressions surface as bubbles. Just now the words "*Staten Island Advance*" bubbled up in my mind. I don't particularly want to talk about that newspaper because I hardly remember anything about it. What I do remember is that I was once on the front page when I jumped out a third-story window. It was just a small article, no picture: "A twenty-four-year-old man [had my name] fell from a window at such-and-such address in St. George today. As he was standing by the open window, he suddenly felt dizzy and fell out." That's all it said. It did give me credit for having survived such a fall, though.

This is a painful memory and I have told bits of it before. I was on LSD at the time and I thought I had become transcendental. I broke both heels when I landed, and believe me, if you have broken heels, you don't walk on them, but I walked on mine, my imagination flying. I was seeing myself as a throwback to primitive society before the human race was civilized. My hallucination was so complete that I accepted it as reality. I wasn't some guy who had just fallen out of a window and broken his heels; I was an atavistic being who could walk despite pain. Cave men could ignore pain because they were so brave and their lives were so hard that pain was nothing to them.

Right before I walked out the window, I had been reading the *Upaniṣads* of all things. I was disoriented and confused because reading the *Upaniṣads* and taking LSD are a bad combination. It was written in the *Upaniṣads* that matter was insubstantial and that only spirit was real. That led to my wanting to prove my spirituality by walking out the window.

I remember reading one devotee's account of "How I came to Kṛṣṇa consciousness." He said that when he first read Prabhupāda's books, he was trying to understand the difference between matter and spirit, and the idea that matter is unreal and spirit is real. He got up and walked into a wall. He said, "I bumped my head." Then he tried again and bumped his head again. I wonder if he thought he could transcend the wall and walk right through it by understanding that he was not his body. This is a stupid form of literalism. I had made the same mistake.

My mind was also full of guilt at the time, guilt for my recent activities, guilt for how I was living, guilt for the fact that I had been associating with destructive and immoral people. Walking out the window had something to do with that too. It was almost a call to show my courage. Did I have enough courage in my convictions to walk out a window? Yes, I did. I know all this sounds strange as I pour it out.

If you want to come down to earth, to use a painful metaphor here, and give all this a Kṛṣṇa conscious context, I'll say this: I was headed for death, but His Divine Grace saved me from the insanity brought about by hallucinogenic drugs. I had been brought up with middle-class morals, but I had rebelled and was living a degraded life. His Divine Grace saved me from that too. He saved me from my guilt, and he saved me from my unhappiness. The memory is what it is, but the real essence is that Prabhupāda was kind to save me.

# This Self In This Body Who Has Lived This Life

A student at the University of Buffalo once asked Prabhupāda, "When you go inside yourself deeper and deeper, within and *within*, what do you find?"

Prabhupāda replied simply, "That you know. I do not." Then he said, "The self within." If we look deep enough, we'll find the pure spirit soul. When we see that pure form of ourselves, all the other, self-created selves will fall away.

All devotees know this and that's why they are reluctant to talk about any part of themselves that might not be that absolutely pure and Kṛṣṇa conscious person. The only truth is the spirit; there is nothing else worth discussing.

It's not only devotees who think like this. The Māyāvādī says, *brahma satyaṁ jagan mithyā:* spirit is truth, the universe is false. Yes, we see varieties of flowers—orange ones, yellow ones, roses, and blossoms on trees—but the sense that each is different is an illusion. The Buddhist says that neither the varieties nor the plants themselves exist in truth. Well, do they exist or not? Being presented with such a frustrating picture of ultimate truth, we usually find ourselves falling back to what we know: this self in this body who has lived this life.

It is nine o'clock in the morning. The sky is clear and the cows are grazing in distant pastures. The last remnant of a white moon sits in the sky and the flies are already becoming pests. We sit to think, to remember, just like anyone else, but we have an abiding belief that everything comes from God. We chant Hare Kṛṣṇa.

Why don't we use our time to remember something we read about Kṛṣṇa? Because we are looking for Kṛṣṇa in our own lives and because it is stated in the *Bhāgavatam* that we should make prayers in order to make our speech chaste.

# Overcoming Regrets In My Relationship With Śrīla Prabhupāda

When I was Prabhupāda's personal servant in 1974, I felt restless and wanted to go and preach in America on his behalf. I confessed this to him one day. His response was stern. He said my idea was whimsical and that I should not "jump like a monkey." I felt bad that I had even asked to change services and to leave his side. I apologized and asked him to please always keep me in his service.

But I couldn't give up the desire to leave. I expressed my feelings to Tamāl Krishna Mahārāja, Bhāgavat dāsa, and others, and they all assured me that I would get some relief when we left India and started to tour Europe. I didn't feel relief in Europe; the desire to leave Prabhupāda's personal service and return to America remained.

Then one day, in a room full of GBC men, Prabhupāda began to discuss the importance of forming a traveling party to distribute his books to the college libraries in America. There was no one to do it, so I volunteered. Prabhupāda turned to me and said, "Then do it."

I left his room elated. I recorded my feelings in my diary. I was surprised that my desire had been so easily granted, although it turned out not to be so easy. A replacement had to be found for me, and although the most likely candidate was Brahmānanda, he had important duties in Africa. We were in another European city (I don't remember which) when Prabhupāda raised the topic again. It was during his massage. As I began the massage, he asked me about the library party and I said that the men were enthusiastic about my joining them. Then Prabhupāda asked whether or not Rūpānuga could lead the party. It was a crucial moment. I felt that Prabhupāda wanted me to stay with him and therefore was suggesting that someone else could lead the party. Of course, Prabhupāda wasn't sentimental or attached to me as his servant, but he was practical. Rūpānuga was already in America and I was already serving him. I said no, I didn't think Rūpānuga could lead the party, and I gave a good argument: it didn't seem likely he would be able to travel constantly with the men because he was a *gṛhastha* and a temple president. Was I really so concerned about the distribution of Prabhupāda's books in America, or was I more interested in joining the team of *brahmacārīs* again and being freed from the confining routine of being Śrīla Prabhupāda's servant?

I confessed to Karandhara how I was bored sitting in the other room all day waiting for Prabhupāda's bell to ring. Karandhara sympathized and compared it to a fireman who spends most of his time waiting for the alarm. When the alarm finally rings, his role becomes important.

I remember all this with regret, especially that moment when Prabhupāda asked me whether or not Rūpānuga could do the library party service. That was the moment I could have retracted my request. To hell with the idea that I was the only one who could lead the library party in America! It would have gotten done one way or another. For that matter, Prabhupāda's personal service would have gotten done one way or another too, but I lost my chance to be his servant. It is likely that as far as Prabhupāda was concerned, I could have remained his servant for the rest of his days.

I know it's a useless regret for me to keep chewing on, but it obsesses me. I just wasn't simple and affectionate enough toward him to stay. I remember when we thought of Brahmānanda as my replacement, Prabhupāda said, "Yes, he likes my company." That comment still stings.

Now Prabhupāda is celebrated all over the ISKCON world as the greatest personality, the purest devotee of Kṛṣṇa, and anyone who has memories of being in his association is considered fortunate.

The question I ask myself today is more penetrating than the usual run-through of this memory. I am asking myself why, although it was obvious that Prabhupāda wanted me to stay with him, I wanted to leave. I can say that I was meant for service in separation, but is there also an implication that I didn't love him, and that being too close to him I saw that he was not a person who inspired me? Was I bored with his lecturing on the same basic topics? Was I sometimes hurt and put off by the strong way he dealt with people so absolutely? How he got so much involved in management and also seemed to want me to get involved? Was his temperament too different from mine?

Why is it that I craved my own space so much? Why didn't I bathe more in the rays emanating from his person? Sometimes I think I could have survived those days if I had kept a diary, but that diary might have been more an outpouring of my own doubts and the craving I was experiencing to be my own man than a discussion of Prabhupāda's pastimes.

Perhaps it's best not to tear myself apart with regret. It's certainly not good for me to find fault in Prabhupāda. The abiding truth is that I do wish to serve him. Whatever talents I have I wish to use in the service of his movement and mission. I want to repeat his teachings. If I don't fit perfectly like a glove on his hand, I still wish to be enlisted in his army. Maybe I'm in the outer reaches, but I'm definitely with him, and whatever gains I make will be dedicated to his service.

There are some things that if Prabhupāda had asked me, I couldn't have surrendered to. If he had asked me to become the temple president in an Indian temple or to distribute books in India, I know it would have been hard to surrender to those requests. I might have agreed at the time but found myself incapable of really doing the service later. I guess there are limits to surrender. The basis of it is always to stay as Prabhupāda's devotee. Fortunately, Prabhupāda knew this and accommodated our sincere desire to serve him despite our limits. Sometimes he asked too much of one servant or another, and although he may have expressed some initial disappointment when that servant failed, he would allow us to take a second-best position. If we flourished in that position, he would always express his acceptance of and pleasure at our service. We had to swallow the reality of our limits, of not being dearmost, of not being the most surrendered, of not being capable of loving him as much as we wanted to, and it was hard, but it didn't change—and it doesn't change—the fact that he is the one who saved us. It was he who showered us with affection. We never want to leave his service.

# Why I Don't Dwell On Controversial Memories

Last night, Madhu read to me the chapter about Prabodhānanda Sarasvatī from O. B. L. Kapoor's book, *The Gosvāmīs of Vṛndāvana*. It seems that Prabodhānanda Sarasvatī's life is shrouded in mystery and the book discusses the possible reasons why he was not mentioned or quoted by the other Gosvāmīs of Vṛndāvana. Some scholars even raise doubts about his authorship of *Rādhā-rasa-sudhānidhi*. The Vallabha *sampradāya* may have themselves authored that book. By the end of the chapter, I felt not completely satisfied, which is not how I felt when I read the chapter about Raghunātha Bhaṭṭa Gosvāmī. I realize that in one sense, it is necessary to hear the different opinions—we shouldn't be naive or too simple in our understanding of the different personalities in Gauḍīya Vaiṣṇava history—but on the other hand, there was too much wrangling instead of straight *kṛṣṇa-kathā*.

It occurred to me that the equivalent could take place a hundred years from now if scholars write about the various arguments and controversies that concern ISKCON today. A future reader could get completely absorbed in the controversies and miss the actual quality of life that we are leading now. Worse still, *we* could become so absorbed in the various controversies that we miss living the quality of life that Prabhupāda has offered us. We're usually so close to the events as they happen and so filled with the emotions that arise in their midst that we have no objective vision anyway. Although there is certainly value to subjective recollection, we should realize that subjectivity does not paint the complete picture. Therefore, I prefer not to discuss the controversies. They will pass.

Saint John of the Cross wrote about this topic. He said that in these times of rocky seas, he wanted to cling to something solid in life: his devotion to God. The steady factor in my life is whatever sincere devotional service I can offer to Śrīla Prabhupāda. That is most worthy for me to remember. Just this morning I heard Prabhupāda telling how the boy Nārada Muni was blessed by the *vedāntavādīs*. Prabhupāda said that anyone who serves a pure devotee, the spiritual master, or a Vaiṣṇava by eating the remnants of his food or washing his dishes or cleansing his feet will get spiritual benefit. We don't have to become Vedic scholars; by our rendering service, Kṛṣṇa will automatically reveal Himself in the heart.

Fortunately, I have been given many opportunities to realize the import of this statement in this lifetime, and they are most worthy of remembering. Even if I also remember the awkward moments with Prabhupāda, the mistakes I committed and the ways in which I failed, such memories are still within the context of living in his grace. Although I have been offensive and have fallen short, as long as I try to be obedient and to follow my nature as his disciple, he doesn't kick me away.

What I call "controversies" or things that are too troublesome to discuss are actually different forms of not being simple and straight in service to guru. I can own up to my own participation in some of the controversies in ISKCON and see them for what they are, but I prefer not to dwell on them. They don't disqualify me from returning to the simple life where I belong. No one has done anything so wrong that he cannot be forgiven and accepted back into simple service to the *sampradāya*.

# Tuscarora Creek

I remember looking out my window at the cabin that was my home by the Tuscarora Creek. The creek was an olive-drab color much of the time, and I found it attractive as it reflected the trees' light. Usually it was a slow, lazy creek, with not even enough water in it to row a boat, but after a heavy rain, it would course like a river. Then people would row by, Pennsylvanians on holiday. It always startled me to see them go by, rowing through our private land as if they had a right.

The creek seems to be something from my past, just one of the things I have renounced or that has renounced me. It was dear to me, but like so many things, our coming together was coincidental and doomed to end. I remember Paramānanda saying how special it was to live by a creek. He said that people who didn't live by a river didn't know how important it was. I was glad that he was sensitive to my feelings and that he also liked the natural setting, the seasons and moods of a creek.

The creek was frozen in winter, the tree boughs on the bank hanging over it, heavy with snow. I took many walks on the back road that runs parallel to the Tuscarora. Often I would sit in a particular place to watch the creek and hear it coming around the bend. It was always peaceful, and it soothed the stress of GBC management and Gītā-nāgarī pressures. I felt I was with Kṛṣṇa in nature.

But bit by bit I renounced it. Now it will never be the same. The house in which I lived is now too big for me and I no longer lay claim to it. I'm not the emperor of far-flung lands I used to be where I could claim large rooms for my personal use. I don't feel bad about it, although I reserve a special place for it in my memory.

# Vocation As A Writer

When I was a teenager, it began to occur to me that I should become a writer. The intimation came partly from something within myself and partly from the acknowledgment I received from others for my writing. It was the first thing I had done for which I received real acknowledgment. No one had ever told me I could become a great ball player or that I was a born military leader, but they encouraged me to write.

William Carlos Williams said that he decided to become a poet after an illness which was so debilitating that he could no longer pursue his dream to become an athlete. Williams was a great writer, with a long and dedicated career. We would expect his first meeting with his vocation to have been more romantic, but that's not always how it goes. Vocations are sometimes vague in the beginning, and our motives may be mixed in wanting to follow them. It was like that in my case. It's not that I suddenly became enamored with the idea of becoming a writer; it was more a gradual falling in love with the craft.

When I was young, I wrote short stories. My theme was often something from my life: the story of a young man who wanted to become an artist. I was also excited by good writing and often modeled myself after the writers I liked. For example, I liked Kerouac, especially his descriptions of himself as Sal Paradise, and I began to write in my own notebook in a similar way. Writing was a joy for me, and I loved to compose vignettes and impressions and share them with my friend, John Young.

In those vignettes, I nurtured my identity as a writer and an artist. My definition of "the artist" didn't always coincide with what was expected of an artist in the bohemian '60s, however. I remember Tommy Oakland, a friend, saying behind my back that a mutual acquaintance of ours, a flamboyant painter who was boldly living with his girlfriend, had more of "the artist" in his little finger than I had in my whole body. That remark didn't hurt me because I realized that I defined "the artist" by different criteria.

To me, it didn't matter whether an artist was a bohemian or not. An artist was someone who practiced his art, who studied the art of others, and who dedicated his life to improving his art. A writer worshiped art and kept trying his hand at it. It was a serious, lifelong commitment, and I planned to take it seriously, not just because someone praised me, but because it was what I was.

I started my writing career by keeping a diary. This is also around the time that I read *Catcher in the Rye* and began listening to Jean Shepherd on the radio. I also discovered beer. My life was burgeoning with new feelings and experiences as I grew to see myself as separate from my parents and to express a yearning for going beyond their world. My diary was full of frustration and dreams.

I still remember that first diary. I wrote with an Esterbrook fountain pen in a loose-leaf binder. I was inexperienced in many ways, but I craved romance. At the beginning of the diary, I pasted a photograph of a young man and woman sitting on a bench under a blossoming cherry tree. It symbolized an ideal state to me. I also had a photo of a soldier charging toward the camera with his bayonet. This was to express my anti-military feelings. Under it I wrote something I think I had heard Jean Shepherd say, "Wither goest, O mankind." That diary grew thicker and thicker as I wrote, usually at night or whenever I wanted to be alone with myself.

When I went to college, my professors thought I was a good writer and gave me encouragement. That's when I started writing short stories for the first time. At Brooklyn College, I took two creative writing courses, and during two successive semesters, I won first prize in contests for the best written piece in the college magazine, *Landscapes*.

Then I went into the Navy and later moved to the Lower East Side from one tenement building to another. I lost various possessions—my books and articles. I kept my diaries at my parents' home on Staten Island, but they too were eventually lost. None of that mattered to me much. The books I cared about most I destroyed soon after meeting Swamijī. Those were several short novels.

One was called *Green and Golden*, and it was an attempt to fictionalize my relationship as a young boy with an outlandish but lovable family figure, a shy Irishman named Jimmy Duncan. That was mostly fiction and didn't seem to have much real heart in it. Another short novel was called *The Avocado Theme*. In this I tried to express my being a young man on Staten Island with my friends and how we grew up to aspire after a Kerouacan kind of life. That story ended with my friends going to hitchhike across America while I decided to stay back.

Then I wrote a short novel called *Sagittarius*. I wrote this while under the influence of marijuana. The chapters were improvised and allegorical, and they included scenes from the Navy and the Italian ports I had visited, an allegory about a man climbing the Statue of Liberty and having a sense of Brahman realization at the top. Much of it was done in imitation of various masters, but my goal was to express my own frustrations through symbols. I actually sent *Sagittarius* to a publisher, but received a rejection notice.

One of the best things I wrote was a short story about our dog, Mickey. Through Mickey, I was able to describe my family life. Some people—including my sister, Madeline—thought that this story proved my talent more than anything else I had written.

The last thing I wrote before meeting Prabhupāda was a semi-fictional autobiography about a character named Svevo. It was about life on the Lower East Side, a romance with a girl there, drug experiences, and the pain of a sensitive person growing up in that tough environment. I included a lot of poetry and a sincere description of the Lower East Side in the 1960s. I brought that work through a number of drafts and felt it was something dear because I had written it out of the blood and tears of my own life.

Writing dedication was my religion. I had nothing else in life—no girlfriend, no decent job, waning youth, and no happiness. I had been willing to sacrifice everything for writing. I was willing to be a martyr for art, a mood I learned from Kafka and Van Gogh.

When I met Prabhupāda, I didn't throw out the writings immediately, as I did my record albums. When I first moved from my apartment on Suffolk Street into my "devotee" apartment on First Street, I started fresh, but I took my writings with me. They were so integral to my identity.

And my identity followed me. I had sent *Svevo* to an underground publisher in Chicago and he wrote back saying that he thought the writing was "superb." He wanted to publish it in installments in his magazine. In fact, I spoke to Swamijī about this and asked him if I could write a sequel to tell how Svevo had come to Kṛṣṇa consciousness.

Prabhupāda approved, but added, "They should not give you less money because you are religious." I remember being happy that he approved of me writing, but I never did write that sequel. It just didn't seem part of the same life that the Svevo book represented.

Throwing my writings away was my idea; I never discussed it with Swamijī. One day I walked toward the storefront and it clicked that it was something I had to do. My writings were my greatest attachment and I had to give them up. This was my preliminary—and not very mature—idea of something called "renunciation." I knew I was supposed to renounce whatever was unfavorable to my Kṛṣṇa consciousness. When I faced what I could see as the truth about my writings, I admitted that they were not Kṛṣṇa conscious. They were also a great attachment. They were a credit to my "genius," a proof of my being an artist. Therefore, better to destroy them and to become a humble servant of the Swami and nothing else.

In 1966, I told Hayagrīva that I would never write again. He and I were still only acquaintances, but I knew he was a college professor and that he also wrote poetry. I thought he would know about literature. When I told him that my writing was false, he expressed something different. He said he didn't think writing itself was false, but that he was going to write for Kṛṣṇa.

I wasn't convinced then. One day I carted all my carefully typed manuscripts—hundreds of pages of everything from *The Avocado Theme* to *Sagittarius* and *Svevo*—and walked to the storefront. Instead of going into the storefront, I went in the main door which led to the apartments, and instead of walking through the building to the rear where Prabhupāda lived, I went to the incinerator and dumped all my writings in. And that was that.

# Why I Didn't Become A Father

Dīna-dayārdra dāsī asked, "Did you and your wife ever consider having children?" That's a frank and perhaps inappropriate question to ask a *sannyāsī*, but I think I'll answer it. Dīna-dayārdra herself has two beautiful little redheaded, freckle-faced boys, and she lives in a family-oriented community where they are strict about raising their children as part of their devotional service.

Although I don't think much about it, I guess a person without children is an object of interest to those who have children. Sometimes, people with children even pity those who have never parented. Some people even see it as a destruction of the family line. Although that's another thing I haven't really thought about, I guess that's what will happen to my family line, at least as it extends from my father. My father had a son, and he would have expected me to have a son. But I didn't. That's the end of the Guarino line.

That was also true of Henry David Thoreau. The Thoreau family worked hard to come to America and to survive the harshness of those days, to establish the family on American soil, but Thoreau had no children and that was it. The family line died out. I can see why in many cultures, not having children is seen as a lack of responsibility. It is an act of selfishness. In Thoreau's case, he just didn't do his family duty. In their eyes, he frittered his life away selfishly and didn't continue the dynasty. At the same time, the Thoreau family has become a permanent entity in American history. As long as there is America, there will be the Thoreau name. Although Henry David didn't have children, he created a kind of "spiritual" family who continue to read him through the centuries.

Cāṇakya Paṇḍita says that a home without children is void. In the Vedic conception, a male child (*putra*) is important because he can liberate his forefathers from the hellish existence of disembodied life after death. Therefore, children are important.

Now let me answer Dīna-dayārdra's question directly. The information is already contained in the collection of Prabhupāda's letters. I was married on Bhaktivinoda Ṭhākura's appearance day in September of 1968. In October, I wrote to Prabhupāda and asked him how one goes about conceiving a child—what time of the month are we supposed to try, etc. Prabhupāda replied that it was not really proper to ask this question of a *sannyāsī*, but because we were so dependent on him, he agreed to answer it. We were planning to have children, but just after receiving this letter, a plate glass window fell on my head and we had to wait. Shortly after that, my wife got sick. That created another delay. Then I wrote to Prabhupāda and asked whether we should try to have children at all. My wife wasn't yet clear of the debilitating illness, and Prabhupāda said that if the mother was sick, the children would also be weak.

These are the circumstantial reasons why we never had children. In addition, our marriage was quite a renounced one. We were both serious devotees. Prabhupāda has sometimes said that unless the husband becomes the servant of the wife, married life cannot be peaceful. She also has to become his servant. Neither of us became the servant of the other. We just didn't have a compatible and deep husband-wife relationship. We both sensed that underneath such a relationship, it was *māyā*. I tried and she tried, but I was certainly more interested in my temple president duties and she was only interested in painting. Sometimes we would go through throes of feeling we should be more attached, but more often we felt detached and thought our only business was to follow Prabhupāda's instructions and just do our service. When she was inclined to have a husband, I was more interested in taking care of all the devotees, not just her. The pendulum swung back and forth. Any time we engaged in any tinge of sense gratification, we would both be immediately repelled and the pendulum would swing the other way. We were not living a peaceful *gṛhastha* life.

By Kṛṣṇa's arrangement, we entered into an unofficial *vānaprastha* stage when my wife went to New York with the art department and I stayed in Boston. Later I went to Dallas and soon after took *sannyāsa*.

I have lived many years with no opportunity to produce children, but I don't feel barren. I don't know what it's like to have children. I suppose it can be satisfying. From this side, it looks troublesome. It takes so much energy to raise a child in Kṛṣṇa consciousness, and even then the results are not guaranteed. The children often don't remain serious devotees and the parents are left brokenhearted. Just as I have been spared attachment to a wife and to my parents, so I have been spared attachment to children, which Madhumaṅgala says is the most binding of all. Still, I have spiritual sons and daughters, which although not exactly the same, Prabhupāda considered better.

# Proud Of Prabhupāda

One devotee told me that she once bought a lemonade from a man in front of the Krishna-Balaram Mandir in Vṛndāvana. He asked her who her guru was. When she told him my name, he said, "Yes, he is a *sādhu*!" She felt a childlike pride. Then she asked if I remembered any moments when I had felt that same childlike pride in Śrīla Prabhupāda.

I felt it when I went from office to office, person to person at Harvard University trying to get Prabhupāda an appointment as a faculty lecturer. People didn't praise him, but I felt that pride.

Then when he came and lectured, he looked so great. I hoped the students would appreciate him. I love it when someone says, "He is a great spiritual master. He is the one who came to America and started the Hare Kṛṣṇa movement." I've always liked that story (although I heard it only third-hand) of the little black woman in a Manhattan grocery store who heard Prabhupāda's name mentioned and said that she had read about him. "He came to America with no money. He was so brave!"

"Śrīla Prabhupāda, I'm proud of you." Such a simple thing to feel. We almost feel we're not entitled to feel such pride in Prabhupāda. Who are we? But yes, we can be proud, just as we are proud of our worshipable Lord Kṛṣṇa, the Supreme Personality of Godhead, who spoke the world famous *Bhagavad-gītā* and danced the *rāsa* dance.

# Spiritual Fantasies In The Early Days

When I first began to chant Hare Kṛṣṇa, passing the beads through my hands, I felt like an ancient sage—I have written about that before—but did I seriously think I was actually a sage in 1966? Did I have a spiritual fantasy life in those days or try on different personae to see which one fit? Did I dare to wear these personae in front of Prabhupāda?

Whatever little games I and the others played were examples of our gross neophytism. Prabhupāda smashed them quickly and easily with just a glance or a word. For example, I once sat in front of him in a pseudo *āsana*, my thumbs and first fingers touching. Prabhupāda looked at me with such displeasure that I immediately realized the ridiculousness of what I was doing. When you sit before someone as powerful as Śrīla Prabhupāda, you don't pretend you are self-absorbed. Rather, you cross your legs or sit in a lotus or a half-lotus and just listen to whatever he has to say. If you're intelligent enough, you also ask questions. Another time I asked Prabhupāda if he thought Chinese philosophy was advanced. He said no and that ended another fantasy I was carrying: I couldn't be a Chinese sage in front of him either.

I did know that I had many persons and subpersons in me and that I had to choose which one was the one

Kṛṣṇa preferred. This was something I had thought of even before I met Prabhupāda. I expressed it to him once in a complicated, "mental" way. I thought that there was no real person within us, but that we could make up different ways to be by donning different masks or costumes. I thought we did this just to please and impress someone else. Therefore, to please and impress the Supreme Lord, what person should I be? After all, wasn't it in my control to pick and choose among my many personae? When I remember that question now, I realize how elusive and weird it was.

Anyway, Prabhupāda replied to my question by saying, "This boy, Steve, is nice. He gives money and he types. You should also do like that." I loved that reply. It touched my heart deeply because Prabhupāda had defined the person he wanted to see. That is, be plain, gentle, a disciple who is willing to work. Keep your head out of the clouds. He also told me to keep my job at the Welfare office and to be sober. He molded me like that. I went to work and gave him my paycheck to help his mission. I chanted on my beads in that context, not thinking I was a hoary second-generation Vyāsadeva walking the Lower East Side. Although I continued to wear Western clothes, gradually I began to wear *tilaka* to work and to shave my head—all within the context of the identity he had given me. He didn't turn me into something exotic or even something Indian. I didn't become a sage who chanted continuously, but a young man who worked within his limits, gave money, attended the classes, and developed his attraction to Kṛṣṇa in the process.

# He Needs Fighters

I remember eating *purīs* on the verandah when I was Śrīla Prabhupāda's servant. I have told this story before. Rūpānuga's young son said, "You're eating like a voracious wolf." I was offended but said nothing. I also remember eating cold chipped rice, yogurt, and mangoes in 1973 on that same verandah in Māyāpur. Śrīla Prabhupāda wandered out of his room and saw several of us sitting there. He was in a pleasant mood and asked, "Is it nice *prasādam?*"

I liked it when Prabhupāda was easygoing and in a happy mood. One time, however, he sat in his darkened room after the opening of the Krishna-Balaram Mandir and called his leading GBC men to him to express his displeasure that his books were not being printed. He looked cross and even hard. His *kurtā* buttons were gold, but they were undone. Of course, it was his right as guru to express his displeasure as much as his pleasure. Do I always want him to be the sweet guru coming out of his room to ask how the mango and yogurt tastes? It just isn't like that. He can be cross, he can let his face go unshaven because he's not a ladies' man or a TV performer or a politician begging for votes. He doesn't have to show the right profile; his profile is always right. His profile is his entire dedication to Kṛṣṇa. Therefore, he asked us in 1972, "Are you convinced? Unless you are convinced you cannot help me." He needs fighters, just as the U.S. Marine Corp needs dedicated men, not crybabies who feel homesick in India and yearn for grilled cheese sandwiches and 7-Up. He wanted us to stick it out with him, even in Calcutta when the rats roamed freely through the kitchen and were not afraid of us.

Was I ever afraid of Prabhupāda? Yes, I was afraid. I still am. I'm afraid I'm not afraid enough.

# God Remembers

Devotees often ask whether as I go over my memories, I find things about my life in ISKCON or my service to Prabhupāda that I regret. Yes, I regret, but it's not exactly regret. I observe that I fell short. I also see that the movement was tough and imperfect. In other words, I was falling short, but so were others. We were falling short together.

What can I say? The history has already been lived. The leaders (myself included) sent the underlings out to collect thousands of dollars to send to the BBT. That's what Prabhupāda wanted—money to go to the BBT. Still, there was something wrong in our approach. We leaders were proud. We had what we called a "millionaires club," and only those GBC men who turned in a million dollars a year to the BBT were members. Bhagavān was always in the club, and Rāmeśvara, and probably Jayatīrtha. Gopāla Kṛṣṇa Mahārāja made it one year. My biggest year added up to only $300,000, which was huge for me, and I got a little pat on the back, but in order to collect that much, I had to allow the *saṅkīrtana* leader to send devotees out alone to live in motels in American cities, and to go out and sell paintings. Some of them fell down. Or he would send out a husband and wife team for weeks at a time with no association. Their only order was to sell, sell, sell, and bring back the money. There wasn't much attention to their spiritual lives, and some of them fell too.

Sometimes I went out into the field to meet these "traveling parties." I remember one time in particular when I arrived in sub-zero weather in Chicago. We got together in a motel and I lectured on the verses that say we should take the *karmīs'* money and give it to Kṛṣṇa. Rāvaṇa had kidnapped Sītā! We had to bring her home to Rāma. I also gave a lecture from the *Bhagavad-gītā* on Kṛṣṇa's order to fight. You can't be a better moralist than Kṛṣṇa.

Even then someone said, "This just doesn't feel honest. We're presenting these paintings as if they have been painted by American artists, but they are Korean factory paintings." Okay, I said, if you feel that way, then don't go on selling them. But those who persisted were honored and given gifts at post-marathon festivals. We were *all* caught up in this—the whole society.

Is it still going on? I don't know. They seem to have new methods for pushing people to collect for Māyāpur and for the BBT. I don't know whether it's better or worse because I'm no longer part of it. Neither am I one of those vampires who try to drain ISKCON of life, or a blasphemer who tries to unearth all the mistakes and lump everyone together under one label. I only want to remember it here, face it, and both forgive and be forgiven.

I can see people stepping forward upon reading this: "I was thrown out of the temple when you were in charge and it was unfair." Someone said I separated him from his wife or that I lied and cheated. It's not all true. I'm no crook. I did wear silk, which is made from boiling silkworms, and I drank milk from slaughtered cows (store-bought milk), but we all do that and we purify it by chanting Hare Kṛṣṇa. I'm not one of those guys who says that whoever uses an aluminum pot and eats white sugar is a certified demon. After all, Śrīla Prabhupāda was aware of Kali-yuga's built-in imperfections. The main thing is to serve Kṛṣṇa and to try to stay as much as possible in the mode of goodness.

The problem with memory is that it leads us down these murky paths. Once we start, we find ourselves saying, "You're not going to bring *that* up, are you?" Then we're sorry we started remembering the past in the first place. We just wanted to remember Śrīla Prabhupāda coming out of his room and seeing us eating mango and yogurt; we just wanted to remember the time he smiled at us in 1966. But what comes up? The very worst, and some of it isn't even true. We shut the Pandora's box and turn to Prabhupāda's books, but the lid doesn't quite close and the bad smell is leaking out into the room. It's not that everything can be covered up forever. It's no wonder some people prefer to have amnesia: "I'm sorry, I don't remember that."

All we can pray for is that although the blame is heaped on our heads along with the infamies we didn't commit, God can see all and cleanse us and forgive us. Dear Lord, this is how I lived my life. Now I depend on You to see into my heart. If you find anything good, I know You will remember it.

# Preserving The Record

Caraṇāravinda dāsī remembers being in Vṛndāvana one year and spontaneously celebrating my Vyāsa-pūjā ceremony although I was not there. She writes, "All the boys in our *āśrama* were there. We started with a *kīrtana* and then spontaneously spoke our offerings to you. I think that this spontaneity is what made the occasion special: everyone spoke from the heart a prayer or words of affection for you, their spiritual master. The atmosphere was so uninhibiting that I even managed to say something myself, which under normal circumstances would have been impossible for me. I felt cleansed and purified and everyone else did too. . . . Later, Vṛndāvana-līlā and I made a Vyāsa-pūjā book to send you. We used lots of Indian stencils to decorate it. I really enjoyed making the book with Vṛndāvana-līlā. Do you remember getting it, Guru Mahārāja?"

No, I can't say I remember that particular book right now. I used to get so many books in the mail. Of course, that doesn't in any way negate or minimize what Caraṇāravinda felt and what she remembers now. It does show that in the guru-disciple relationship, the intense feelings expressed on one end may not be immediately received on the other. Disciples sometimes expect that the spiritual master is picking up their affection and surrender by some telepathic means, but it just isn't like that. Therefore, the disciple should be satisfied to make an offering and to feel the purification. If the guru touches our heart and we want to speak our affectionate words even when he's not present, then that act is complete in itself. The communication back and forth doesn't have to occur instantaneously, but can be part of a lifetime of shared Kṛṣṇa consciousness. Rūpa Gosvāmī states that Vaiṣṇavas should exchange *prasādam*, gifts, and intimate thoughts. That doesn't mean we have to always be connected to a telephone line for instantaneous exchange. Sometimes there is a gap of time between when the intimacies are shared one way and then the other.

Caraṇāravinda's memory of her initiation ceremony is also worth sharing. She writes, "I was a nervous wreck during the ceremony, spending most of my time rehearsing the four regulative principles in my mind. I kept going over them again and again while you were giving the lecture. I always seemed to forget at least one of them. When it was eventually my turn to go up, you asked me to repeat the principles. I was so nervous that my voice came out high-pitched like a tweetie-pie or a young child. There was nothing I could do to control it. Everyone laughed at the sound of my voice, which made me hope the ground would swallow me up. Then you smiled and said, 'If you can practice the four regulative principles as nicely as you can say them, then your spiritual life will be successful.' "

Patrī has a memory that while not the same, reminds me of the same point. He writes: "In 1983 I had stopped living with the devotees in the temple. Pṛthu and Vidura came to see me and I got into the car to talk with them. Vidura then began to drive from Belfast to Dublin. I was horrified to learn along the way that you were visiting the temple. It meant I would have to face all the devotees and you as well. When we arrived, I went upstairs to the temple room. You were just coming out of your room. I paid my obeisances and hoped you would keep walking, but you waited for me to get up. I snuck a look while I was offering obeisances and saw your feet. You were waiting. It was no use. *Praṇāma* prayers can be dragged out only for so long. I was going to have to stand up and face you. I couldn't look you straight in the eye. You smiled and in a playful way, hit the top of my head with your knuckle. 'Knucklehead!' Then your mood changed to a more serious one. You said, 'You have been lucky this time. Don't do this again. You may not get another chance. *Māyā* may swallow you and you'll be lost forever.' Then you walked away. I felt like a total idiot and a fool, exposed for what I was."

I can't remember that either, except in a hazy way. I do remember that Patrī left the association of devotees and that some devotees went to "rescue" him. I also remember being shocked when I heard he had left and glad that he had come back. That was 1983 at the height of the zonal *ācārya* days. I was expected to do certain things, to be on the highest platform of guru. In retrospect, I may say that I was expected to be a figurehead. Someone else was already organizing and inspiring these devotees. That's what I read into these memories now. I would never call someone a knucklehead now, at least I don't think I would, but that was me being heavy, as I was expected to be. And my little speech, "You have been lucky this time"—there's nothing wrong with it; it's a good speech. But it was something I would have been expected to say. I'm a different person now. I was probably still wearing that raw silk in those days, getting even more headaches than I am now, and visiting temple after temple filled with devotees all looking to me as the figurehead. I'm not trying to mock those days, just to try to get at it all.

There were so many incidents, so many fires, so many beads and names handed out. I tried to act as Prabhupāda had trained me. Now I'm smaller, I hope more honest, and freer from pretension. Even if I don't remember that guru who gave a young girl her name or welcomed back a wandering devotee, maybe I felt good about it at the time. Maybe I liked the fact that people laughed and smiled and listened seriously to what I said. I liked to represent Prabhupāda and Kṛṣṇa by performing the *yajña*. I would have searched among the kindling and found a few small pieces to start the fire. Then I would have conscientiously lit it and poured ghee to keep it burning. I would have said the mantras, gotten a headache, done the whole bit. Afterwards I would have washed my hands, sat back, had a laugh, shared a joke, and looked forward to *prasādam*. Is that so bad or demoniac?

It occurs to me while I'm thinking about these things that the extremists who attack ISKCON have put me on a kind of permanent defensive. It's similar to what the anti-cult movement did to us in the 1970s. I took the anti-cult movement personally and I don't think I've been the same since the irate parent groups formed national and international networks and began to attack our movement with lies and exaggerations and smears. The extremists are a more insidious group because they are able to make more hurtful and sometimes truer accusations, if still exaggerated or taken out of context. Such people make it harder for me to make honest criticisms of myself as guru because as soon as I attempt to make what sounds by comparison to be a mild confession, I hear them jumping on it, taking advantage of my statement to use it against me and others.

I shouldn't let them frighten me, or worse, silence me. In years to come, all this will just look so foolish that we won't even want to remember it. In the meantime, I can preserve the record.

# First Impressions of Prabhupāda

Two different devotees asked me about my first impressions of Prabhupāda. Hare Kṛṣṇa dāsī then described how she had first met the man who would later become her husband. She said she attended a lecture he gave at the Belfast temple. As she sat in the back of a crowded room, he made no deep impression on her, although now she looks up to him and they have a deep and cooperative relationship as they raise children and a garden. He's become her *pati-guru* in a way I find admirable. She says, however, that as a Western woman, she has always had the expectation of love and romance in the back of her mind, and that wasn't part of their meeting.

Then she described how she first met me, the person who was to become her spiritual master. She says she had a lot more expectation and anticipation in that meeting because I was the sole initiating guru for Ireland at the time. By then, she had also learned enough about Kṛṣṇa consciousness to know the importance of the guru-disciple relationship. Also, I was delayed in coming to Ireland for months because I had been living as an invalid at Gītā-nāgarī. Therefore, when I arrived at the temple in Ireland, everyone was filled with anticipation. At first she was in the back and couldn't see me, but when she did manage to see me, she said she felt something strong because she knew she would be accepting me as guru. She already planned to have a first impression. She was not so prepared when she met her husband.

This was her introduction to her question: what impression did I have of Prabhupāda the first time I saw him? Did I have any inkling that this person would become the one around whom I would center the rest of my life? Did I know that he would rescue me?

I can't even remember the first time I saw Prabhupāda. I guess that answers the question indirectly because it must mean that I didn't have a deep first impression. That first sight of Prabhupāda has become lost to me in the general and gradual coming to him over the weeks at 26 Second Avenue. As time went by, I did become very attracted to him, and I certainly felt the true and affectionate guru-disciple relationship develop. I also very much respected him, although I was a hip twenty-six-year-old from New York City, full of the sophistication of Western culture and education. When I met Prabhupāda, I was into my own self with all my concepts of Western intellectualism. I was an artist and that was a whole identity in itself. Prabhupāda was, at least externally speaking, so different from me that I don't remember there being a complete crashing of barriers or an electric shock realization leaping from him to me upon our first meeting.

I approached Prabhupāda for a human relationship and I respected him. I didn't like to hear the devotees joking about him behind his back, for example. I thought that anything he did was to be taken seriously, even his quaint Indian behaviors and his way of expressing himself. But it was not a romantic encounter of love at first sight; we had to cover so much distance to get to know each other. Therefore, I tend to think that my own experience discredits the importance of romantic first meetings. What's more important is that the relationship built up bit by bit, moment by moment, and that it continues to do so.

# Young Friends

I remember eating fruit salad and *mahā* cookies in the afternoon at the Chicago temple. I was the GBC then. The temple president told me that he didn't know how much relevance I had to his temple. Of course, he was right. I didn't know what to do, especially since he didn't look up to me or want whatever contribution I could have made. In contrast, I had a sweet and affectionate relationship with the temple president in Houston, Lakṣmī-Nārāyaṇa Prabhu. His temple was small and not so successful, but we loved each other. One year at Māyāpur he spoke to the Berkeley temple president, who was much more successful. Both temples were part of my zone. The Berkeley temple president later remarked to me that Lakṣmī-Nārāyaṇa was a real small-timer because his big excitement was getting up early and chanting rounds with the *brahmacārīs*, as if this was the stuff of success. I was hurt by his comment because I shared that same vision of success. Chanting was *my* idea of fun and vitality too.

O Lakṣmī-Nārāyaṇa Prabhu, I know you left ISKCON years ago, but I'm sure that if we ever meet again, you would remember those times in Texas when you and I were young and friends.

# I Shouldn't Be Here

When I arrived at the temples in my zone, devotees would gather and greet me with a *kīrtana*. In the Northeast U.S. I drove around in a 78 Oldsmobile. Remember? I'm sure some of you do.

In Vancouver, Bahūdaka used to roll out a red carpet right across the parking lot and into the temple. Near the end of those days, my headaches overwhelmed me. How had I sunk so low? What was wrong with me anyway? The doctors were filling me with a variety of medications and then Dr. Sarma came with his Hindu Nature Cure. I was grateful to receive what I thought then was The Answer.

That same year, the zonal *ācārya* system crashed to the ground. It started with the epic meeting at New Vrindaban. I went, but couldn't attend all the sessions. One day I saw one of my Godbrothers. I said, "I shouldn't be here," meaning that my health was so poor. He replied, "*None* of us should be here." His remark hurt because he didn't address his reply to my illness. I realize now, though, that it is impossible for a sick person to expect reciprocation, and especially in a situation like that when I was one of eleven zonal gurus —the cause of all the problems. Yes, no one should have had to be there.

During that period of convalescence I learned to love nature and the land of Gītā-nāgarī. It was a nice time in that regard, the closeness to nature. Sometimes I'm sorry I can no longer see the seasons change at Gītā-nāgarī; I was enriched by those days and my walks down the dusty back roads of summer.

I no longer have a home base. I have learned to like the novelty of new places. It keeps them from becoming dull. Thomas Merton says just the opposite. He says if you live in the same place for a long time, you get to witness it in all its seasons. Every twig and tree takes on personal significance. It seems for now that I'm still meant for traveling around—if Madhu ever gets the van together, our tiny, claustrophobic world. How long will that go on? I'm only fifty-seven years old, still young.

# Free Spirit

One devotee asked me, "Can you remember how you felt when you first shaved your head and wore Vaiṣṇava dress and *tilaka*? Were you seen as partisan? Did it seem at odds with your free-spiritedness? Did you feel you were being shackled by party spirit? How did it affect your writing? Did you feel as if you were nailing your colors firmly to the mast?"

That's an odd expression, "nailing your colors firmly to the mast." Yes, it occurred to me that because ISKCON had its own party spirit and vocabulary, and because I equated it with the way the Marxists created solidarity among their members, that now I was identified as a devotee. I wasn't wielding a Marxist's vocabulary now, but a Vedic one. I didn't mind. I was willing. My definition of "freedom" was flexible, and whatever else I had tried had not brought me happiness thus far. The *Śrīmad-Bhāgavatam* redefined "free spirit" as someone who lives in Kṛṣṇa and who can escape from the material frame once and for all. Although the Lower East Side intellectuals scorned my leap of faith, I remained silent but repeated the philosophy to myself. For example, I said, "Everything comes from Brahman."

"What the hell is Brahman?"

I didn't have to answer. It was a premise of my "new religion" that I was willing to accept simply because the Swami said so. Up until that point, I have been living with scraps of knowledge but little belief, no faith. We were speculators, but what did we know? We lived only for sense gratification. Now I had found the Supreme.

One apostate, fifteen years after having left the institution and its disappointments, said, "I will live without ultimate answers as does most of humankind nowadays." He thought we were foolish to live in a cloud of absolute certainty regarding matters that we could not prove. That's his world now: orthodox views not permitted. All free spirits must sail their own boats.

Well, I climbed into the Vedic boat and have no desire to abandon ship. O poet of self, don't live in Whitman's abstract dream. You are eternal and there is no need to fear.

# A Lesson

Guru-sevā dāsī wrote, "I remember a meeting I had with you. I was talking continuously and really absorbed in my mind. I looked up and saw you looking straight past me through the window behind. You had noticed something in the field beyond, perhaps a low-flying hawk, and your attention was focused there. I could hear the hollow echo of my words and they suddenly seemed so small. That moment was like a Zen experience. Everything seemed contained within that fragment of time and my self-absorption contrasted with the actual path of *bhakti*. In that moment I was jolted into the understanding that real self-absorption means to aspire for genuine concerns, not the peripheral, mental ones that go round and round. It was a lesson that helped me mature at a time that I needed to mature, and I felt that your looking past me at something beyond was a lesson you were personally teaching me."

I imagine my Godbrothers, peers, or critics looking at this memory and trying to apply objectivity to it. Was the guru *actually* teaching a lesson or not? Or maybe the disciple is just so submissive (or naive) that she has read more meaning into the meeting than the guru was capable of giving.

Objectivity aside, I wonder what people would think if a disciple of Prabhupāda told this story? Of course, because of Prabhupāda's spiritual stature, we could assume that he *did* intend to give that instruction, but it's also possible that he saw a low-flying hawk and it caught his attention, or that he was so intensely thinking of Kṛṣṇa that he barely noticed the devotee in front of him. (There is a story about Rūpa Gosvāmī like that.) What's my point? That a disciple's submissive mood creates favorable exchanges.

# Those Days And These

Praghoṣa dāsa asked me to again assign value to living in the 1966 days with Prabhupāda. He put it like this:

> In 1966, ISKCON seemed so sublime. It not only had a single purpose but a single method of achieving that purpose, and this personally guided by Prabhupāda. Everything seemed simple, straightforward, and anxiety-free, the devotees cocooned in a warm secure world protected by Prabhupāda. ISKCON 1996 seems to have many purposes and many ways of achieving those purposes. It seems complicated and even troublesome at times. We seem to have as much to fight about among ourselves as we do with the *karmīs*. How much do you miss 1966, having experienced both eras?

It's hard to answer a question in terms of "how much." How much do you love me? I immediately thought of the words of that old pop song:

*I love you a bushel and a peck*
*a bushel and a peck and a hug around the neck*
*a hug around the neck and a barrel and a heap*
*a barrel and a heap and a talkin' in my sleep,*
*about you, about you.*

How much do I miss those days? I don't even know if I do miss them. I know that there's no possibility of going back to them. I do certainly remember them, and I know that they are the foundation of my present Kṛṣṇa consciousness. If we take the beginning of spiritual life literally as if it were a second birth, then I had a good birth and upbringing. My spiritual parents (guru and the *Vedas*) were always kind and affectionate toward me. Later in my life, as I grew up, I didn't get as much attention from my spiritual father, but those formative years were mine to remember and to give me strength of purpose. They continue to serve me in my extended life of service in separation after Prabhupāda's disappearance. As Praghoṣa put it with eloquence, ISKCON is now a troubled and multipurpose movement. I can float on the waters of that turbulence because I can remember that the essence, after all, is what it always has been: chanting Hare Kṛṣṇa and serving the spiritual master.

How much do I miss those days? How much do I love my spiritual master? That will be tested by my ability to endure the present. Life isn't always so heartwarming or simple, but staying true now becomes another way of staying true to the earlier days of my spiritual life. Someone who was so privileged as to have been there in those days should not be quick to observe our present frailties and quit. Let me remain, even if I am diminished. Let me be a witness to the continuum of Prabhupāda's purpose.

# Blurred Neons

A devotee asked me about something he said he read in one of my books, although I cannot remember the incident. He said, "You spoke of leaving your world behind for Swamijī. You met with a friend and told him of your new discovery, but he couldn't appreciate it. You said tears welled up in your eyes, and as you traveled back to your apartment, the neon signs of stores and offices and the traffic lights seemed blurred in your vision." He said the image of me as a young man leaving the material world behind moved him whenever he thought about it.

I don't remember any teary farewells with the material world, but I do remember two final partings. One was when my friend Murray and I parted company. I liked Murray. He was a good man. Even when the other artists we knew became degraded, he kept an air of goodness about him. I looked up to him as a superior writer and poet.

I had invited Murray to the storefront at 26 Second Avenue to share my discovery. After the lecture, we went out together and walked around the Lower East Side trying to find some friends home. I remember ringing different doorbells that night and not finding anyone home. As we walked, I began to sing one line from *Westside Story*, "Stick to your own kind, one of your own kind." That's the song the Puerto Rican family sings to advise Maria not to fall in love with a non-Puerto

Rican. I hadn't intended anything by it, but Murray snapped angrily, "Then why don't you stick to your own kind if that's what you want?"

His words were right to the point and it was true: this would be the last night that I would attempt to span two worlds. He also said, sarcastically, "So what should we do with our precious time?" It was a stinging comment because up until that point, we had not thought of time as anything precious. Now, however, I had discovered some meaning to my life, that I could chant Hare Kṛṣṇa and live every moment in devotion to God. I had discovered that because we are eternal, life is imbued with an eternal purpose.

Finally, he suggested that we go to a local bar where many hip people congregated. I didn't want to go. He kept walking toward the place anyway and I held back. Then he turned and made a gesture of farewell. At that moment, his face and form froze into a tableau for me. The moment was so surcharged with final parting that it made an impression. It was like one of those avant-garde films that end by freezing the last frame to produce a shock effect. Time froze for me for a moment, then released me, and we parted.

The other parting was with someone named Richie. Richie and I weren't close friends, but because he was now living in the Second Avenue area, I told him about the new scene. Hare Kṛṣṇa was hip enough that I could introduce it without becoming embarrassed. I told him that I was practicing this mantra and that it got me higher than LSD. He listened with interest, but I don't remember much more about that meeting. What impressed me was what happened after I left him.

Although I rarely took taxis, I took a taxi from his apartment in Greenwich Village to the Lower East

Side. As I drove through the streets, I remember feeling deeply that I was leaving an entire world behind forever. I was moving into a new world. It was as if there was now no return to everything that I had known—the life of long-haired, bohemian dissoluteness, the way Richie was living with his latest girlfriend, the way he was so weak-willed, wasting his time smoking marijuana, so unclean, so devoid of God consciousness.

I don't remember tears and blurring neons. I do remember one other time when I saw those neons, though. I was already practicing Kṛṣṇa consciousness full-time. I went to a program at a club where we were chanting Hare Kṛṣṇa in front of our Viṣṇu painting. I became suddenly bored and walked away, thinking that I didn't so much like the association of those people who were devotees. When I walked into the streets and saw those neon signs and stores and the people walking around aimlessly, I became frightened and returned to the devotees. They were just coming out of the club and I ran to join them, hoping they would forgive me for my having momentarily strayed away. Of course, they did, and there have been no blurred, teary neons for me.

# Not Better Nor Worse

I want to be a true devotee of the Lord and of my spiritual master. I am following my Guru Mahārāja and that will have to be good enough for me. I am one of his crew. I have described, and I continue to describe, how I sometimes feel estranged. I have also described how I have gone through trips and changes and that I continue to do so.

I let my mind jump like a monkey this morning while I was reading *Kṛṣṇa* book. We all do that from time to time, but the mental concessions we give ourselves are just little forays. We'll be back. There's no point pretending. We are not better or worse than we are. It's wrong to follow whimsy and weakness, to follow someone other than our spiritual master, but we make these forays because we are not able to fully appreciate him. We sometimes think his teachings are too basic or that we have read them too many times to be able to sustain a fresh interest. The fact is, however, and we know this to be true, that his books give us Kṛṣṇa's *darśana*. No one else is going to do that for us. We have to surrender to *some*one, the true teacher of *dharma* who comes into this world to save us. We have done that. Let's grow and be ourselves in his service. It's only right. And yes, we can admit our doubts and troubles along the way. There's no point in pretending to be perfect or even fully satisfied.

This morning I went into the *tulasī* house in Uddhava's backyard. They have the most beautiful *tulasīs* I have ever seen—six of them in big pots and simply covered with purple *mañjarīs*. Madhu says he can smell their fragrance even outside. I take off my shoes outside the house, enter, bow down, and recite the prayers, "*Vṛndāyai tulasī-devyai* . . . " I always read the translation posted on a placard hung on the wall: "O Tulasī, beloved of Kṛṣṇa, I bow before you again and again. My desire . . . " I don't have it memorized, but it feels good to read it. Then I feel the cold, hard cement creeping up from the soles of my feet and my daily headache begins to announce itself. I feel sincere when I recite the prayers and see those *mañjarīs*. Thank you for this moment.

Afterwards, I go and pick raspberries and another berry Uddhava says is a cross between a blackberry and a raspberry. I pick about twenty of them for my breakfast. It's a simple thing and I like to do it. Then I go back to my routine, digging up as many memories as I can.

Let's be truthful, be devotees, stay with the master, read his books. Be your own best friend. Dear Śrīla Prabhupāda, thank you for helping me to remember you. Thank God for the devotees who see me as your servant and who ask me to speak of my time with you.

# How I Wish To Be Remembered

He asked, "How do you wish to be remembered?" I wish to be remembered accurately. I wish to be remembered as a conditioned soul who wrote in his present, struggling state to help other conditioned souls. I wish to be remembered as someone who didn't hurt devotees by such writing, but who simultaneously purified himself and offered the same opportunity of purification to others. I don't want to be remembered as someone who had already attained purity. I don't want to be remembered as someone who could not be trusted, who was a misleader or mundaner, someone who would detain others. It should be accurate.

Some writers are so honest about themselves that they think they shouldn't be remembered because their association was useless to others. For example, Kafka told his friend, Max Brod, to destroy his writings after he died. He didn't think they would help people. I don't feel like that at all. I *want* my books to help others; I write them to help others.

They ask me to remember. I say I can't remember worth a damn. I stood or sat in the padded pews and heard Gospel readings every Sunday. I didn't always understand what they were talking about—something about someone sowing seeds in a vineyard. It grew and someone was supposed to take care of it. What was the point? Something about a man who was hired for a full day's work and who was paid the same wages as someone who was hired for half a day. The full-day workers complained to the master about the unfairness of being paid the same amount as those who worked so much less, but the master told them not to complain. Weren't they satisfied with the wage they were offered at the beginning of the day? Yes? Then they shouldn't complain. The master had the right to pay his workers however much he liked. The priest said it meant there was a different kind of justice in the kingdom of heaven.

The Gospel reading the week before Easter was especially long. Mostly I thought my own thoughts and examined the shape of the priest's hat and vestments, the frill of lace at the bottom and at the cuffs. I looked over the altar boys in their white, lacy smocks as they held candles and rang bells. I don't think I knew any of those boys intimately, and sometimes the priest got curt with them for making mistakes. One priest (was it Father Farricker or Father Flannagan?) got so angry that he threw his black hat across the altar. They asked for donations, and my father, who didn't attend Mass, complained that the priests were always asking for money. I heard it all and I still remember it.

"The children are listening."

"Little pitchers have big ears."

I couldn't assimilate it all, but some of it stuck as the smoke rose from the bluish-red glow of the cigars under the lamplight.

Do I remember? Yes, I remember. I also remember my ISKCON days, the Swami and my Godbrothers and Godsisters and the things I have told a million times. All I have is Prabhupāda's *mūrti* now. He is kind and doesn't demand too much of me and I like him as he looks at me. I plan which *cādars* to offer him and I still massage him daily. It is a compensation.

# A Last Recognition

Near the end of Prabhupāda's pastimes, I went into his room and prostrated myself before him. Although in the past eleven years, he had always welcomed me affectionately, this time he wasn't communicating with us. In April and again in August of 1977, I journeyed to Vṛndāvana to be with him. We would go into his room and sing soft *kīrtana* with a pair of tiny *karatālas*. When I took the lead one time, he said no, he wanted Haṁsadūta to lead.

Did that crush me? Yes. Brahmānanda dāsa was there and later said that it must have been difficult for me to travel ten thousand miles to be with Prabhupāda and then for him to interrupt my *kīrtana* so Haṁsadūta could sing.

It was hard, but later I was leading the Nṛsiṁhadeva prayers during his very last days in November. He didn't stop me that time, but asked Tamāl Krishna Mahārāja who was singing. Tamāl Krishna Mahārāja leaned down and spoke my name into his ear. Prabhupāda said, "Mmmm." That was his last recognition of me. All disciples want that, I know. Prabhupāda was kind enough to give it to me.

# Little Life

I just saw the van drive off. Madhu has gone to weigh it. Praghoṣa went with him in case Madhu feels too weak to drive. He has been sick. The van's travails go on and on, seemingly without end. I can't keep up my anticipation about our travels. I simply have to wait.

This house has been shrouded in gloom the last few days—all the curtains are closed and Madhu has been lying in bed. I have not been able to play the tape recorder in the bathroom in the morning for fear of disturbing him, and I tiptoe up and down the stairs, keep the light off, and don't ask him for news. Everything has been put aside while he recovers.

I am supposed to receive a phone call at noon today from our doctor. I'll tell him that this week was better than last. The little life. It's all we have. That, and our connection to the great, unlimited sky of Kṛṣṇa's pastimes. How high can we fly in that sky? How much can we remember? What is the quality of our *smaraṇam*?

When we remember the great descendent of the Yadu dynasty, do tears come to our eyes? When we remember Govinda standing by the Vaṁśīvaṭa, are we stunned? Do we no longer desire to return to family and friends and their mundane jokes? Do we remember Lord Kṛṣṇa's instructions in *Bhagavad-gītā* and feel strong in heart? Queen Kuntī wanted the Lord to stay with her always, and when the *gopīs* remembered Kṛṣṇa, there was no end to their emotional transformations. Even nature shared those transformations. Do we remember our guru and cry? Well, those states are all beyond me.

Kṛṣṇa is the Supreme. My lessons are over. This is my last day here and I am another day older and deeper in debt, moving through time.

My spiritual master was especially kind to us and gave us the best instructions. Sometimes he reprimanded us and sometimes he was encouraging. He walked with us in the morning in Māyāpur and on Juhu Beach. He was the undisputed chief of ISKCON. People may claim power and righteousness in his name these days, but when he was walking on the beach, no one claimed anything, and if they did, he could correct it in a moment. I remember him. I remember serving him and traveling away from him to serve on his behalf. I remember reading his books in those simpler days.

Tomorrow we leave. We are fortunate to be in this river of important considerations called the Kṛṣṇa consciousness movement. Anywhere we dip in, we come up with a handful of Ganges water. Don't sell it short.

# Glossary

## A

**Ācārya**—A spiritual master who teaches by his personal behavior.

**Ārati**—A ceremony of worshiping the Lord by the offering of various auspicious articles, such as incense, flowers, water, fans, ghee lamp, etc.

**Āśrama**—A spiritual order: *brahmacārī* (celibate student), *gṛhastha* (householder), *vānaprastha* (retired), *sannyāsī* (renunciate).

## B

**Balarāma**—Kṛṣṇa's elder brother and His first plenary expansion.

**BBT**—Bhaktivedanta Book Trust; the publishing house solely and exclusively authorized to publish Śrīla Prabhupāda's books.

**Bhakti**—Devotional service to the Supreme Lord.

**Bhāva**—The stage of transcendental ecstacy experienced after transcendental affection.

**Brahmā**—The first created living being and the secondary creator of the material universe.

**Brahmacārī**—A celibate student living under the care of a bona fide spiritual master.

**Brāhmaṇa**—Those wise in the *Vedas* who can guide society; the first Vedic social order.

**BTG**—Back to Godhead magazine.

## C

**Cādar**—A shawl.

**Caitanya (Mahāprabhu)**—Lit. "Living force." An incarnation of Kṛṣṇa who appeared in the form of a devotee to teach love of God through the *saṅkīrtana* movement.

**Capātī**—A whole-wheat, griddle-baked flatbread.

## D

**Dāl**—A spiced bean soup.

**Darśana**—Vision; audience.

**Devakī**—Kṛṣṇa's mother in Mathurā.

**Dhāma**—Abode; the Lord's place of residence.

**Dharma**—The duties prescribed by one's nature and social position; ultimately, *dharma* means devotional service to the Supreme Lord.

**Dhotī**—Vedic men's dress.

## E

**Ekādaśī**—A day on which Vaiṣṇavas fast from grains and beans and increase their remembrance of Kṛṣṇa. It falls on the eleventh day of both the waxing and waning moons.

## G

**Ganges (Gaṅgā)**—A sacred river in India that washed the lotus feet of Lord Viṣṇu.

**Gauḍīya Vaiṣṇava**—A follower of Lord Caitanya.

**Gaura**—A name of Lord Caitanya Mahāprabhu, meaning "golden."

**Gaura-Nitāi**—Lord Caitanya (Gaura) and Lord Nityānanda (Nitāi).

**GBC**—Governing Body Commission, ISKCON's board of directors.

**Gītā-nāgarī**—A spiritual farm community established by Śrīla Prabhupāda in Central Pennsylvania.

**Goloka**—Kṛṣṇaloka, the eternal abode of Lord Kṛṣṇa.

**Gopī**—A cowherd girl; one of Kṛṣṇa's most confidential servitors.

**Gṛhastha**—A married person living according to the Vedic social system.

**Gulabjamon**—A sweet ball made from milk powder, fried in ghee, and soaked in sugar syrup.

## H

**Halavā**—A sweet dish made from roasted farina, butter, sugar, and water or milk.

**Haridāsa Ṭhākura**—A great devotee of Lord Caitanya Mahāprabhu; known as the *nāmācārya*, the master who taught the chanting of the holy names by his own example.

**Harināma**—Public chanting of the Hare Kṛṣṇa *mahā-mantra*.

# I

**ISKCON**—Acronym of the International Society for Krishna Consciousness.

# J

**Jagannātha-ratha**—A chariot (*ratha*) on which the Deity of Jagannātha rides, used in a festival celebrating Kṛṣṇa's return to Vṛndāvana from Dvārakā.

**Janmāṣṭamī**—The festival of Kṛṣṇa's birth.

**Japa**—Individual chanting of the Hare Kṛṣṇa mantra while counting on beads.

# K

**Kali-yuga**—The present age, which is characterized by quarrel and hypocrisy.

**Kaṁsa**—A demoniac king who tried to kill Kṛṣṇa during His childhood pastimes.

**Kaṇṭhi-mālā**—Beads worn around the neck by devotees of Kṛṣṇa.

**Karatālas**—Hand cymbals used during *kīrtana.*

**Karmī**—One engaged in karma (fruitive activity); a materialist.

**Khādī**—Homespun cotton cloth.

**Kīrtana**—Chanting of the Lord's holy names.

**Kṛṣṇa**—The Supreme Personality of Godhead.

**Kṛṣṇa-kathā**—Topics spoken by or about Kṛṣṇa.

**Kurukṣetra**—A holy place where the war between the Pāṇḍavas and the Kurus took place and where Lord Kṛṣṇa spoke the *Bhagavad-gītā* to Arjuna.

## L

**Līlā**—Pastimes.

## M

**Mādhurya-rasa**—Devotional service to Kṛṣṇa in the mood of sweetness and conjugal love.

**Madhvācārya**—A thirteenth-century Vaiṣṇava *ācārya* who preached the theistic philosophy of pure dualism.

**Maṅgala-ārati**—The first Deity worship of the day, performed an hour and a half before sunrise.

**Mathurā**—The city where Lord Kṛṣṇa appeared and to which He later returned after performing His childhood pastimes.

**Māyā**—The external, illusory energy of the Lord, comprising this material world; forgetfulness of one's relationship with Kṛṣṇa.

**Māyāpur**—A town in West Bengal, India, where Lord Caitanya appeared.

**Māyāvādī**—An impersonalist or voidist who believes that God is ultimately formless and without personality.

**Mleccha**—A class of persons outside the social and spiritual divisions of Vedic culture, whose standards and practices are considered abominable.

**Mṛdaṅga**—A two-headed clay drum, traditionally used in *kīrtana*.

**Mūrti**—A form, usually referring to a Deity.

## N

**Nanda**—Kṛṣṇa's father in Vṛndāvana.

**Nārada Muni**—A great devotee of Lord Kṛṣṇa who travels throughout the spiritual and material worlds singing the Lord's glories and preaching the path of devotional service.

**Nārāyaṇa**—The four-handed expansion of Lord Kṛṣṇa.

**New Māyāpur**—A spiritual village established by Śrīla Prabhupāda in rural France.

**New Vrindaban**—A spiritual village established by Śrīla Prabhupāda near Wheeling, West Virginia.

## P

**Pāda-yātrā**—A traveling missionary festival, conducted mainly on foot.

**Paramparā**—The disciplic succession of bona fide spiritual masters.

**Parikrama**—A walking pilgrimage.

**Pati-guru**—Lit. "husband-spiritual master." A term of respect addressed to a man by his wife.

**Prabhupāda, A. C. Bhaktivedanta Swami**—Founder-ācārya of ISKCON and foremost preacher of Kṛṣṇa consciousness in the Western world.

**Prajalpa**—Foolish, idle, or mundane speech. Talks unrelated to Kṛṣṇa consciousness.

**Prasādam**—Lit. "Mercy." Food which is spiritualized by being offered to Kṛṣṇa, and which helps purify the living entity.

**Pūjārī**—A priest, specifically one engaged in temple Deity worship.

**Purī**—A deep fried, puffed bread.

# R

**Rādhā**—*see Rādhārāṇī*

**Rādhā-Govinda-Mādhava**—The presiding Deities of ISKCON's New Māyāpur community in France.

**Rādhārāṇī**—The eternal consort and spiritual potency of Lord Kṛṣṇa.

**Rāgātmikā**—The spontaneous devotional mood of the inhabitants of Vṛndāvana, according to their loving attachment.

# S

**Sādhana**—Regulated spiritual activites meant to increase one's attachment to Kṛṣṇa.

**Sādhu**—Saintly person.

**Samosā**—A savory, deep-fried pastry, stuffed with vegetables and/ or curd.

**Sampradāya**—A chain of disciplic succession through which spiritual knowledge is transmitted.

**Saṅkīrtana**—The congregational chanting of the holy name, fame, and pastimes of the Lord.

**Sannyāsa**—Renounced life; the fourth order of Vedic spiritual life.

**Sārī**—Vedic women's dress.

**Śāstra**—Revealed scripture.

**Siddhānta**—The perfected conclusion according to Vedic scriptures.

**Smaraṇam**—The devotional process of remembering the Lord.

**Śreyas**—Activities which are ultimately beneficial and auspicious when performed over time.

**Śrīmad-Bhāgavatam**—The *Purāṇa*, or history, written by Śrīla Vyāsadeva specifically to point to the path of devotional love of God.

**Swamijī**—Lit. "Great master." A common term of respect addressed to *sannyāsīs*.

## T

**Tenth Canto**—The part of the *Śrīmad-Bhāgavatam* describing the most confidential pastimes of Lord Kṛṣṇa.

**Tribaṅga**—Lit. "Bent in three places." Refers to the three curves of Lord Kṛṣṇa's posture as He plays upon His flute.

**Tulasī**—A great devotee in the form of a plant; her leaves are always offered to the lotus feet of the Lord.

**Tulasī-mālā**—Beads used for chanting, made from the wood of the sacred *tulasī* plant.

## U

**Uddhava**—A confidential friend of Śrī Kṛṣṇa in Dvārakā.

**Upaniṣads**—108 philosophical treatises that appear within the *Vedas*.

## V

**Vairāgya**—Renunciation.

**Vānaprastha**—Retired life, in which one leaves home and travels to holy places in order to prepare for renounced life; one of the four Vedic social divisions.

**Vasudeva**—The father of Lord Kṛṣṇa.

**Vāsudeva**—The son of Vasudeva, or Śrī Kṛṣṇa Himself.

**Vedāntavādī**—A follower of Vedānta, or one who knows Kṛṣṇa perfectly.

**Vedas**—The original revealed scriptures.

**Vigraha**—Lit. "Form." Refers to a worshipable Deity.

**Vipralambha**—Ecstasy in separation.

**Viṣṇu**—An all-pervasive, fully empowered expansion of Kṛṣṇa.

**Vṛndāvana**—Kṛṣṇa's personal abode, where He fully manifests His personal qualities.

**Vyāsadeva**—The original compiler of the *Vedas* and author of the *Vedānta-sūtra* and *Mahābhārata*, and the author of the *Śrīmad-Bhāgavatam*.

**Vyāsa-pūjā**—Worship of the spiritual master, who represents Śrīla Vyāsadeva, on his appearance day.

**Vyāsāsana**—A special, elevated seat, reserved for the speaker of *Śrīmad-Bhāgavatam*.

## Y

**Yadu dynasty**—The dynasty in which Lord Kṛṣṇa appeared.

**Yajña**—Sacrifice.

**Yamunā**—A sacred river in India, which Lord Kṛṣṇa made famous by performing pastimes there.

**Yaśodā**—Kṛṣṇa's mother in Vṛndāvana.

## Z

**Zonal ācārya**—A now defunct title which conferred exclusive spiritual authority to designated gurus over defined geographic zones.

# Acknowledgments

I would like to thank the following disciples and friends who helped produce and print this book:

Anurādhā-devī-dāsī
Baladeva Vidyābhūṣaṇa dāsa
Caitanya-dayā-devī dāsī
The Friends of Gītā-nāgarī Press
Guru-sevā-devī dāsī
Kaiśorī-devī-dāsī
Keśīhanta dāsa
Lalitāmṛta-devī dāsī
Madana-mohana dāsa
Mādhava dāsa
Madhumaṅgala dāsa
Nārāyaṇa-kavaca dāsa
Tulasi-priya devī dāsī
Vegavatī-devī dāsī

Special thanks to Rupa-Raghunātha dāsa for his kind donation to print this book.